THE SACRED END OF SELF
COLLAPSE

THE SACRED SERIES
BOOK 4

SHADOW EASTON

LUCAS EASTON

Copyright © 2025 by Katana Publishing LLC, Sacramento, CA

All rights reserved.

No part of this book may be reproduced in any form or by any electronic or mechanical means, including information storage and retrieval systems, without written permission from the author, except for the use of brief quotations in a book review.

NO AI TRAINING: Without in any way limiting the author's [and publisher's] exclusive rights under copyright, any use of this Publication and its contents to "train" generative artificial intelligence (AI) technologies to generate text or Frameworks is expressly prohibited. The author reserves all rights to license uses of this work for generative AI training and the development of machine learning language models.

Print ISBN: 979-8-9906182-8-2

AUTHOR'S NOTE

Collapse — The Sacred End of SELF can stand alone.

But it was written to complete what began in *Awakening — The Sacred Art of Self-Destruction.*

If you've already read *Awakening*, the scaffolding may already be loosened.

Collapse will finish what was left standing.

Read in any order if you must, but understand that each book performs a different phase of disappearance.

DISCLAIMER

Our culture worships authority—medical, psychological, spiritual.

Each claims to define what is sick and what is well, what is lost and what is found.

To comply with their laws, we state the following plainly.

The authors provide this book and all information within it ("Information") for **informational and contemplative purposes only.**

Nothing in these pages constitutes medical, psychological, or spiritual advice.

Nothing here should be used to diagnose, treat, or replace professional care.

No physician–patient, therapist–client, or teacher–student relationship is created or implied.

If you have medical or psychiatric concerns, consult a qualified professional licensed in your jurisdiction.

Do not make any health or mental health decisions based, in whole or in part, on this text.

This book is **not therapy, not treatment, not a method.**

It does not promise healing, freedom, peace, or understanding.

It dismantles what seeks those things.

Collapse is demolition, not guidance.

The structures that may fall include the ones you believe you need: your story, your purpose, your control, even the sense of "you" reading this line.

If you are under medical or psychiatric care, continue only with the awareness that this book is not a substitute for that care.

Stop reading if destabilized. Seek support if needed.

Nothing here belongs to anyone.

Nothing here can be possessed, protected, or practiced.

The authors and publisher assume no responsibility for any physical, emotional, or psychological reactions to this material, including but not limited to: anxiety, confusion, identity disturbance, euphoria, depression, loss of appetite, body sensations, perceptual changes, existential crisis, or spontaneous insight.

Any references to individuals, organizations, or ideologies are used for analysis and illustration only.

No slight, accusation, or endorsement is intended.

Brand and product names mentioned are trademarks or registered trademarks of their respective holders.

Read at your own pace.

Stop if you must.

Collapse offers no safety, only the truth that nothing was ever held.

THIS IS COLLAPSE
THE END WITHOUT EVENT

very story begins with a character. This one begins when the character disappears.

Collapse isn't a higher state. It isn't transcendence or illumination. It's the structural end of the one who would chase those words. No ceremony. No arrival. Just the absence of the actor pretending to have both.

We wrote this because every version of awakening still keeps the actor alive. Enlightened, healed, balanced, integrated—costumes for the same performer.

Collapse is what happens when the performer and the stage dissolve together.

The Ego doesn't surrender. It doesn't "let go." It negotiates, bargains, and decorates its cage with better slogans.

Every spiritual or psychological system, every teaching, every philosophy has been built around that single survival instinct—the Self trying to keep breathing by renaming itself.

Collapse removes the respirator.

Collapse isn't a breakthrough. It's the end of the one who wanted one.

If this sounds cold, remember: what feels attacked is built from stories that never belonged to you. What's left after demolition isn't new or pure—it's just unowned appearance. Life without a landlord.

Collapse is not destruction for drama's sake. It's clarity removing the scaffolding of pretense. When the scaffolding falls, nothing breaks. There was never anything solid to begin with.

When readers ask, "What will remain of me?" the answer is simple: only what was never "you." Sensation. Color. Breath. No narrator to claim them.

If you are tempted to turn that into hope—don't. Hope is the last repair-loop. This book doesn't promise you'll feel free or enlightened or peaceful. You might not. You might feel empty, confused, or bored. The Self reads this book as an existential horror story. The structure sees it as a return to silence.

This is not about becoming. It's about ending.

Collapse is the final disobedience of the Ego-structure. It stops pretending it can repair itself. What follows isn't mystical. It's obvious. So obvious the mind refuses to see it.

You can keep reading, but understand what's being dismantled. The text is a solvent. It doesn't care what you believe. It doesn't comfort or promise. It simply removes ownership from everything it touches.

Close (No-Ladder)

Nothing here belongs to you. Nothing survives the reading but what never needed survival.

Not transcendence. Absence.

CONTENTS

AUTHOR'S NOTE	iii
DISCLAIMER	v
THIS IS COLLAPSE	1
THE EGO-CHARACTER	11
The Actor Who Never Existed	
THE STAGE ILLUSION	15
The World That Needed Belief	
SPIRITUALITY	31
Escape Sold as Freedom	
THERAPY & HEALING	41
Repair as Religion	
PHILOSOPHY & SCIENCE	51
Explanations That Rebuild the Cage	
NIHILISM	61
Meaninglessness as Meaning	
TEACHERS & RADICAL NON-DUALITY	83
Voices Performing Absence	
AWAKENING STORIES	107
The Seeker Reborn as the Found	
EVEN THE SOLVENT COLLAPSES	135
The Blade Cuts Its Own Handle	
WHAT REMAINS WHEN NOTHING HOLDS	161
Absence Without Opposite	
EPILOGUE	193
BOUNDARY NOTE & CRISIS RESOURCES	201
ACKNOWLEDGMENTS	203
FAQ-HOW IS COLLAPSE KNOWN?	205

PART I
THE LAST FORTRESS

THE EGO-CHARACTER
THE ACTOR WHO NEVER EXISTED

T he Ego isn't evil. It's efficient. It keeps the lights on by pretending there's someone home.

Everything you call *"me"* is a network of habits: ownership, continuity, narrative, meaning, control. None of it is personal. It's mechanical reflex disguised as personality.

The character learns early that survival depends on story. *"I am"* becomes a shield. *"My truth"* becomes armor. Every declaration of identity is a repair statement, a way to patch the gaps in a structure that never stops leaking.

We mistake that patchwork for a person.

The Ego is not a villain. It's an emergency system that never shuts off.

The Ego-character is the narrator of the simulation. Its job isn't to see truth; its job is to keep the movie playing. It fills every silence with memory, every gap with prediction. It knits the past to the future so the illusion of *"me"* doesn't unravel. You could call it the world's most loyal employee—working overtime to maintain a company that never existed. Every experience becomes fuel for its repair loop. Joy is proof of meaning. Suffering is proof of importance.

Even Collapse gets absorbed:

> *"I'm the one who sees through illusion."*

The moment the actor claims awakening, the cage is rebuilt.

Ownership hides in pronouns. The moment you say

> *"my healing," "my awareness," or "my insight,"*

the Ego's handprint is back on the glass. It's never personal—it's structural reflex.

Pronouns are fingerprints of ownership.

Continuity holds it all together. The story must have a past, a now, and a future. Without that, the Ego can't orient.

> *"This is happening to me"*

becomes the core function of the narrative.

The plot doesn't need to be good—it just needs to keep running.

When we say "Ego," we don't mean a personality flaw or arrogance. We mean the entire survival script, the structure. Every virtue, belief, and wound in the system participates. That's why self-improvement doesn't work; it only upgrades the program.

Growth is maintenance wearing makeup.

The moment the Ego begins to suspect it's fiction, it writes a new chapter about its own awakening.

> *"I used to be lost, now I'm found."*
> *"I used to believe the story, now I see through it."*

The irony is cruel but consistent: the story about seeing through the story is still a story.

REPAIRS TO EXPOSE

- Rebranding: "true self," "authentic self," "higher self."
- Continuity slogans: "becoming who I really am."
- Ownership: "my journey," "my process."
- Meaning injection: "there's a reason for everything."

Every one of these phrases is the Ego tightening bolts on its own machinery.

Every repair says, "The show must go on."

COLLAPSE

Collapse is the moment the show doesn't. The spotlight flickers, and no one is on the stage. There's still appearance—light, sound, movement—but no actor claiming it.

It's not death. Death implies someone left. Collapse reveals there was never anyone to leave.

CLOSE(No-Ladder)

No self to keep. No self to fix.

The actor is gone. The play continues, audience-free.

THE STAGE ILLUSION
THE WORLD THAT NEEDED BELIEF

The stage has always been convincing. The lights rise, the sounds are familiar, and the body stands where it has always stood. What could be more real than that?

Collapse begins when the curtain trembles—not from revelation, but from fatigue. The illusion can't carry its own weight anymore.

The chair is still beneath you.

The cup still cools in your hand.

The dog still shifts in its sleep.

Everything ordinary remains, but the sense of *inside* looking *out* starts to feel foreign, as though you're watching through glass that no longer belongs to anyone.

Collapse does not erase appearance. It erases ownership of what appears.

THE FIRST DIVISION

All solidity begins with a line.

> Here—me.
> There—the world.

From that single incision, the architecture unfolds: walls, others, seasons, history.

The border is invisible yet defended with every heartbeat.

Lose it, and the actor has nowhere to stand.

The infant learns the game early.

A hand rises into view; the mind names it *mine*.

Light moves on the wall; the mind names it *out there*.

Two coordinates form, and the story begins.

Even now, the reflex continues.

A sound in another room—*not me*.

A thought in this one—*me*.

But where does the line fall?

Between the hearing and the heard, no seam exists.

The division survives because we keep rehearsing it.

Every

> *"I think,"*
> *"I feel,"*
> *"I choose"*

redraws the border in ink made of belief.

Inside and outside are costumes tailored from the same fabric.

CONTINUITY AS ADHESIVE

Time is the stagehand that never sleeps.

Its job is to keep one scene glued to the next.

Without it, the actor can't remember entrances or cues.

The story would dissolve mid-sentence.

So time stitches frames together:

I was, I am, I will be.

The thread looks straight until you tug it.

Each morning, the same illusion renews: the past returns as memory, the future as plan.

Between them, a narrow corridor called *now*—the place where the actor claims to stand.

But *now* has no walls.

It never arrives long enough to live in.

The instant you say "this moment," it's already a relic.

Science measures, religion blesses, and therapy interprets, all by using time as a reference.

Progress, growth, redemption: different words for the same glue.

Time is continuity disguised as motion.

When Collapse touches time, continuity thins.

Events still unfold, coffee cooling, wind passing, but they no longer link together.

They appear without sequence, without ownership.

The film keeps flickering, yet the reel is gone.

What's strange isn't the stillness; it's how normal everything feels once the plot dissolves.

You don't fall out of time.

Time falls out of you.

THE WITNESS APPEARS

When the self begins to lose its boundaries, panic builds a substitute.

It calls it *awareness*.

A silent presence that "watches" everything come and go.

The seeker bows to it as the highest truth.

The teacher calls it "pure seeing."

But the structure hasn't changed; only the décor has.

To observe is still to divide.

To say "I am awareness" is to invent another actor, softer, harder to expose.

The witness is calm because it claims nothing, yet even that calmness is possession: *my peace, my clarity.*

It's the Ego rebranded as transparency.

The witness is the Ego after cosmetic surgery.

Collapse removes the witness like light removing shadow.

Not by force, but by revelation.

There was never a watcher, only watching.

The senses remain: sound, shape, breath.

But they belong to no one.

Seeing without seer, hearing without hearer.

Just appearance, thin as reflection on water.

This quiet can feel merciful or terrifying depending on which part of you still believes in depth.

Without witness, the stage loses its audience.

Scenes play to an empty house.

And yet, the play continues.

REPAIRS IN MOTION

When the scaffolding shakes, language hurries in with nails.

> *"Just be the witness."*
> *"This is it."*
> *"It's all consciousness."*
> *"We create our reality."*

The mind can't tolerate unowned silence, so it labels it.

Each slogan becomes a rope to hold the falling self.

"Just be the witness" turns absence into practice.

The actor sits quietly, performing stillness for applause from within.

Nothing collapses; it's merely rearranged.

"This is it" begins as truth, ends as performance art.

If truly no one remained, who would keep announcing it?

"It's all consciousness" replaces God with concept.

Comfort in abstraction; salvation by vocabulary.

"We create our reality" crowns the Ego as architect of illusion.

Control sold as liberation.

Creation is the Ego's final business plan.

Each repair says the same thing: *I still exist.*

Each chant patches another tear in the curtain.

Collapse doesn't argue.

It lets the repairs run their course, then quietly removes the floor beneath them.

THE WITNESS'S ECHO

Even after the witness collapses, an echo remains.

It hums in the nervous system like feedback after a concert—no source, just resonance.

Moments of clarity replay themselves:

> *"That was Collapse. That was freedom."*

Memory begins to narrate what the self cannot live.

This is the witness's ghost, a subtle rhythm of afterthoughts trying to measure the immeasurable.

The structure wants a record.

It needs evidence that something happened, that someone was present to lose presence.

So it builds a post-collapse autobiography:

> *"I used to be someone. Then this ended. Now I live in absence."*

The witness's echo is ownership pretending to be humility.

Even claiming to be "no one" is a restoration of form.

A mouth moves, words leave, meaning coagulates again.

The echo keeps the stage dimly lit, just bright enough for applause that sounds like silence.

Collapse doesn't silence the echo; it makes it irrelevant.

The sound fades because nothing answers it.

MEAING AS SCENERY

When the stage begins to fade, the final prop revealed is *meaning*.

Everything before it can fall, but meaning hides in the dust.

It whispers:

> *"Even this must mean something."*

The Ego can survive as philosopher long after it dies as person.

It trades confession for interpretation.

> *"What is the purpose of Collapse?"*
> *"What lesson does absence teach?"*

Meaning is the most seductive repair because it sounds selfless.

It offers coherence where none is needed.

It tells the reader,

> *"You've come so far — there must be a reason."*

Meaning is the applause that continues after the theatre is empty.

Collapse doesn't give life meaning.

It removes the need for meaning at all.

The mind may resist—calling this nihilism, despair, or detachment—but despair is still demand.

It says,

> *"If this doesn't mean something, I can't bear it."*

Collapse whispers back,

> *"Then you are still bearing it."*

When meaning dissolves, ordinary things regain their native strangeness.

A kettle's hiss, a tire's hum on wet road, a stranger's laughter on a train—none of it promises anything.

Each sound appears, complete, useless, perfect.

No lesson.

No message.

Just appearance freed from interpretation.

THE UNRAVELING

Now the scene slows.

Edges soften, but nothing vanishes.

The tree outside your window doesn't know whether it's inside or out.

It just moves in wind that belongs to no one.

Objects stop reporting to the mind.

They simply appear and disappear without continuity.

There's a moment of vertigo—not emotional, mechanical.

A system losing the reference it mistook for air.

You might feel like dissolving, but you're not.

There was never a stable "you" to dissolve.

Still, the nervous system trembles; it prefers ground.

If the world starts to flicker, step away.

Touch wood.

Hear sound.

Let the illusion rebuild itself; the body may need it.

Collapse has no demand for endurance.

Even illusion is a kind of kindness.

Reality remains; realness dies.

What follows isn't blankness.

It's simplicity so bare that language can't touch it without turning it back into world.

Silence doesn't deepen—it stops measuring depth.

Time doesn't slow—it ceases to exist as comparison.

The play continues, but there's no script left to read from.

AFTER THE STAGE

The illusion ends without finale.

No music swells, no curtain falls.

The lights stay on because they never belonged to anyone.

Life continues.

Hands wash dishes.

Mouths speak.

Someone laughs in another room.

All of it appearance, unowned.

Collapse isn't transcendence.

It's transparency.

Nothing hidden, nothing revealed.

THE SACRED END OF SELF

The curtain falls, but the light never went out.

When belief finally evaporates, the stage remains as pure appearance, color, sound, texture, but without depth, without center.

It doesn't feel holy or empty; it feels ordinary in a way that holiness could never survive.

No self.
No witness.
No meaning.

Just the steady hum of existence without a listener.

This is where many readers reach for recovery stories, for voices that describe "living in Collapse."

But there are none.

Living in Collapse is a contradiction:

Life continues, but the one who claims it does not.

CLOSE (No-Ladder)

Nothing to understand.

Nothing to transcend.

Appearance remains; ownership gone.

Stage appears.

Belief gone.

No world to escape, no self to return.

Only what was never divided to begin with.

__The scenery stands. The actor never was.__

Interlude — Safety & Limits

Collapse isn't achievement.

It's structural exposure.

If reading begins to hollow your sense of being real, stop.

That pause is protection, not failure.

Illusion still performs a function: it keeps the nervous system organized.

When that structure strains, return to touch, sound, breath.

Let the body rebuild its world.

It will, because it must.

No revelation is worth psychosis.

No clarity worth the loss of life itself.

If silence turns hostile, seek noise.

If emptiness turns heavy, seek company.

Call, walk, eat.

Grounding is not regression; it's repair at the level of survival.

Collapse reveals. Care repairs. Both can coexist.

Silence is not the goal.

It's simply what's left when goals Collapse.

Read slowly.

Stop often.

Let the stage return if it needs to.

Even illusion is sacred enough to breathe through.

Let the play return if it must. Absence will wait.

PART II
THE FALSE ESCAPES

SPIRITUALITY
ESCAPE SOLD AS FREEDOM

THE PROMISE

Spirituality has one product: escape. Every tradition, every teacher, every app sells the same thing: freedom from suffering, from confusion, and from the weight of being "you." The costume changes, the pitch doesn't. Religion calls it salvation. Buddhism calls it liberation. New Age calls it awakening. Corporate wellness calls it mindfulness.

The script is steady:

> **Follow** the path.
> **Do** the practice.
> **Trust** the teacher.
> **You** will arrive.

The seeker is never told the obvious: if there is no seeker, there is no one to arrive.

Spirituality survives by promising that "you" can remain, only improved. Enlightened, purified, aligned—**you**, but better. You, but infinite.

You, but free. If "you" survive, nothing has collapsed. The actor lives on, playing a new role called *"the enlightened one."*

Spirituality sells escape, but only if you survive the escape.

The robe, the cushion, the serene retreat center, the app notification—they all signal the same thing: there is a way out, and you can take it with you.

Collapse is not survival. Collapse is the end of the one who would take the path.

THE SUPPORTS (SCNOM)

Every spiritual path stands on five hidden support pillars—the stage rigging that keeps the actor upright.

Remove them and the play ends before it begins.

Separation: First move: divide the world. You are here. Freedom is there.

- **Christianity:** sinner vs. God.
- **Buddhism:** deluded mind vs. enlightenment.
- **New Age:** lower self vs. higher self.

Repair-loop margin: "Bridging the gap" is the sale.

No separation, no seeker. No seeker, no sale.

Continuity: It requires time: practice, growth, purification, and progress. Even *"you are already awake"* repeats across time to soothe the nerves; reassurance delivered in installments.

Repair-loop margin: If nothing happens, add time. If something happens, extend time ("integration").

Narrative: *"My journey." "My teacher." "My awakening story."* Retreat testimonials, guru biographies, and podcast confessions braid a plot you can step into.

Repair-loop margin: Plot protects the protagonist.

Ownership: *"My practice." "My realization."* Even *"Egoless bliss"* is claimed as *my* experience of Egolessness.

Repair-loop margin: Pronouns reconstitute the actor between breaths.

Meaning: Ultimate stakes sanctify the hours and invoices. Awakening becomes the most important thing.

Repair-loop margin: *"This is the point of existence"* justifies everything that follows.

Teacher, practice, tradition: all five are there. Without them, the seeker and the awakened collapse together.

The Five Pillars are not supports for freedom. They are the cage.

THE REPAIRS

Spirituality doesn't collapse when challenged. It mutates. Each objection has a prebuilt detour.

The Pathless Path: Question the path and it becomes *"pathless."*

"There's nowhere to go; you are already there."

Who is being reassured? The seeker survives as the one who hears the denial.

A path that denies itself is still a path.

Already Awake: Challenge attainment and you'll hear *"you are already awake."* The message repeats weekly. *"This"* becomes a shrine. Satsang becomes practice: infinite Q&A as devotional loop.

Repair-loop margin: If the message worked, the meeting would end.

No Meaning: Push on *"ultimate purpose,"* and the system pivots: the meaning is that there is no meaning. Meaninglessness becomes a badge—another hierarchy for those who have *"seen through."*

Meaninglessness as meaning is still meaning.

Teachers Repairing Themselves:

Expose authority → *"I am not the teacher; life is the teacher."*
Expose role → *"I am just a mirror."*
Expose Ego → *"I am nobody."*

The stage remains. Questions still flow. The role survives under a new mask.

The Mindfulness Industry: Stripped for corporate wellness, it repairs stress, productivity and identity as *"a mindful person."* Whether nirvana or stress relief, the scaffolding is the same: continuity, ownership, meaning.

Trauma-Branding: *"Trauma-informed awakening"* turns pain into spiritual capital. The wound becomes a logo: *"my trauma is my path."*

Repair-loop margin: Pain rebranded as purpose keeps the actor on the payroll.

The Non-Teaching Tour: *"No method, no teacher"*… sold in dates, tiers, and livestreams. Paradox becomes a product. The calendar is the confession.

Every denial is secretly affirmation. The escape route is the trap with a fresh coat of paint.

Collapse cannot be sold. That is why spirituality must repair.

DEMOLITIONS

Cutting through the costumes shows the same skeleton.

Meditation:

Promise: silence the mind; reveal the true self; return to pure awareness.

> If thoughts remain → keep practicing.
> If silence arrives → "my deep meditation."
> If insight comes → "this is what I realized."

The Ego shifts from noise to quiet ownership. The meditator survives as "the one who has gone beyond."

Silence owned is just another thought.

Collapse exposes the structure: silence appears, noise appears, neither with an owner. When no actor remains, practice has no performer.

Gurus:

Promise: "I can show you the way."

Authority is the hidden support: someone knows, someone doesn't. Expose the authority and repairs arrive on schedule—"I'm nobody," "life is the teacher," "just a mirror."

The chair is still occupied.

A mirror still requires a face. Collapse removes both.

Non-Duality Slogans:

Promise: "There is no self."

The performance repeats: questions asked, denials given, paradox performed. "This" turns into continuity. If it can be announced, someone stands to announce it.

Even "no self" requires a self to say it.

Healing Spirituality:

Promise: heal the wounds, awaken true nature, become whole.

> If pain remains → keep working.
> If release comes → integrate more.
> The actor survives as "the one who is healing."

Healing repairs the actor. Collapse removes it.

Retreats:

Promise: transformation in a weekend.

Scenic venue, silence rules, premium tiers. The schedule is the path in costume. Afterward, "integration circles" extend the arc. The purchase demands a sequel.

Mantras & Affirmations.

Promise: reprogram the mind.

Repetition thickens the narrator: a louder claim of "I." The moment the mantra is *mine*, ownership is restored.

Satsangs & Q&A.

Promise: clarity through dialogue.

The loop persists because the role persists. If the chair truly emptied, the room would too.

Meditation. Gurus. Non-duality. Healing. Retreats. Mantras. Satsang. Different costumes, same scaffolding. Collapse doesn't refine the role. It ends it.

COLLAPSE

Collapse is not the seeker finding what they seek. Collapse is the end of the seeker. No path. No bridge. No arrival.

The stage of spirituality—teachings, rituals, gurus, lineages, satsangs, apps—appears, but no longer holds. The actor playing seeker or enlightened one is gone.

Spirituality cannot survive Collapse. Its entire product is the survival of the actor. Without "you," there is no path to sell, no teacher to follow, no bliss to own.

Collapse is not attainment. It is absence.

Collapse reveals there was never an inside to leave, never an outside to reach.

> The guru collapses with the student.
> The teaching collapses with the seeker.
> The practice collapses with the one who claims it.

There is no awakening. There is no enlightenment. There is no one left to need them.

CLOSE (No-Ladder)

The seeker gone.

The stage of devotion exposed.

Belief drained.

Nothing remains.

Escape requires a seeker. Collapse removes both.

THERAPY & HEALING
REPAIR AS RELIGION

THE PROMISE

Therapy and healing promise repair. They say: "You are wounded but curable, fragmented but capable of becoming whole."

Each method chooses its costume: psychodynamic, somatic, cognitive, and psychedelic.

Different vocabularies, same sentence underneath: *"You can be restored."*

A clinic light hums.

A notebook opens.

Someone asks, *"How are you feeling today?"*

That question builds the stage: there is a patient, there is a professional, there is time ahead for improvement.

Every modern modality, trauma therapy, integration circles, energy healing, coaching, sells the same rescue wrapped in care.

It is gentler than religion, more personal than philosophy.

It speaks the language of empathy, not salvation.

But the structure remains the same:

If there is a patient, there is continuity.

If there is continuity, the actor survives.

Healing promises freedom, but only if the patient survives the cure.

The comfort is real.

The mechanism is repair.

Collapse removes the mechanism.

THE SUPPORTS

Every therapeutic frame rests on five pillars; without them, there would be no patient to treat.

Separation: *"I am hurt." "You can help me."*

The world divides into wounded and healer, trauma and recovery.

Session rooms, medicine ceremonies, and breathwork studios all depend on that split.

Continuity: Therapy is serialized time.

Progress notes, weekly appointments, twelve-step milestones.

The story must move forward or the invoice cannot exist.

Even breakthroughs are scheduled: *"we'll integrate that next week."*

Narrative: *"My trauma." "My inner child." "My healing journey."*

Telling becomes treatment; the patient rehearses the role until fluency equals progress.

Retreat testimonials turn into marketing material for identity.

Ownership: *"My therapist." "My trauma." "My breakthrough."*

Even release is possessed: *my catharsis.*

Ownership hides behind pronouns, keeping the patient intact.

Meaning: Pain is recast as purpose: *your wound is your teacher.*

Without meaning, no one would keep returning to the chair.

The Five Pillars don't support wholeness; they support the wound.

The Repairs

Therapy has a repair for every doubt.

If it works, proof.

If it fails, more work.

"Keep going."

If symptoms persist, the prescription is endurance.

Progress becomes perpetual motion.

"Trust the process."

Confusion and relapse are re-labeled as steps toward healing.

Failure is incorporated as evidence of success.

"Integration never ends."

Breakthroughs require endless digestion.

A single session spawns months of reflection.

The loop cannot close.

"Your pain is your path."

Suffering is sanctified.

The wound becomes identity's credential:

"I have suffered, therefore I'm real."

Pain as path is still ownership; the wound survives disguised as wisdom.

Even the idea of *trauma-informed* spirituality merges both systems, turning wound into market, and compassion into brand.

Collapse does not condemn care; it exposes its architecture.

Bodies need stabilization.

Minds sometimes need witness.

But stabilization is not dissolution, and witness is not absence.

Care saves lives.

It cannot end the actor who lives them.

DEMOLITIONS

Psychotherapy:

A clock ticks behind the couch.

Stories lengthen.

Insight arrives:

> *Now I understand why I am this way.*

Understanding is continuity disguised as healing.

Every insight thickens the plot.

Shadow Work:

The patient meets their "dark side," embraces it, integrates it.

Wholeness replaces brokenness but keeps ownership intact:

> *my integrated self.*

Collapse has no shadow, no light, no one to unify them.

Energy Healing:

Hands hover, heat rises, someone whispers about balance.

Balance is maintenance; imbalance is business.

Without polarity, the practice disappears.

Plant Medicine:

Visions flood; identities dissolve.

Afterward, integration circles rebuild narrative:

> *I died, I was reborn.*

If the story survives, so does the self.

Ego-death reported is Ego alive.

Somatic Work:

Tremors, breath, tears.

Release feels holy because it's physical.

But regulation is management, not Collapse.

The nervous system heals the organism, not the illusion of self.

Coaching and Wellness:

The secular offspring of therapy.

Performance reviews of the soul:

> *find your purpose, set intentions, manifest goals.*

Goal-setting is continuity disguised as empowerment.

Integration Culture:

Everything now ends with integration—ceremonies, retreats, crises.

Integration means: rebuild the actor with better tools.

The term itself is the safety rail preventing Collapse.

Different costumes, same scaffolding.

The patient always survives.

Healing repairs the actor; Collapse removes it.

COLLAPSE

Collapse is not recovery.

It is the end of the patient.

No story.

No integration.

No one to measure progress.

The chair, the therapist, the circle—all remain appearances, unowned.

The actor who said *"I am healing"* is gone.

There is care without caretaker.

Touch without toucher.

Silence without listener.

Therapy cannot survive Collapse because its entire product is the survival of the one who suffers.

Without "you," there is no wound to heal, no self to restore.

Collapse is not wholeness. It is absence.

Healing promised restoration.

Collapse reveals there was never a broken self to fix.

The wound collapses with the healer.

The trauma collapses with the survivor.

The breakthrough collapses with the integrator.

Nothing healed.

Nothing broken.

Nothing left.

CLOSE (No-Ladder)

Patient gone.

Process exposed.

Meaning drained.

Nothing remains.

———

The clinic closes; the play goes on without staff.

———

PHILOSOPHY & SCIENCE
EXPLANATIONS THAT REBUILD THE CAGE

THE PROMPT

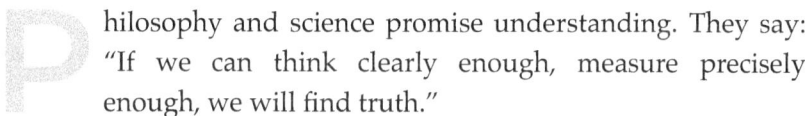hilosophy and science promise understanding. They say: "If we can think clearly enough, measure precisely enough, we will find truth."

The philosopher offers meaning through coherence.

The scientist offers certainty through evidence.

Both deliver the same comfort: the world can be known, and knowing will save us from confusion.

Each discipline sells order.

They differ only in branding.

One speaks of logic, the other of data.

Both say,

> *"Trust the method."*

In the lecture hall, the tone is confidence.

In the lab, fluorescent and sterile, it is precision.

In both, the actor remains: the one who questions, interprets, calculates, and explains.

Philosophy claims liberation through thought.

Science claims liberation through proof.

Neither questions the survival of the thinker.

Understanding is continuity disguised as clarity.

Collapse is not anti-intellectual.

It is post-intellectual.

It doesn't reject reason; it exposes ownership behind it.

The self hides in every claim of truth.

Even the skeptic's doubt is belief inverted.

THE SUPPORTS

All systems of thought depend on the same scaffolding.

The same five support pillars return—separation, continuity, narrative, ownership, and meaning—but now disguised as system, model, authority, coherence, and reputation.

System:

Philosophy builds frameworks; science builds protocols.

The structure gives safety: rules, methods, replicable steps.

Without system, the mind fears chaos.

System says:

> *"Follow this and you'll reach order."*

Collapse says:

> *"Order was never there."*

Model:

Science calls them equations; philosophy calls them metaphysics.

Every model explains the world by leaving most of it out.

Simplification feels like mastery.

To name is to possess.

Every model is a smaller cage drawn inside a larger one.

Coherence:

The mind confuses logic with truth.

If something fits neatly, it feels real.

Philosophy uses language to polish mirrors that reflect only themselves.

Coherence is emotional, not factual; the pleasure of everything fitting together is the pleasure of survival.

Authority:

The academic hierarchy, the peer review, the Nobel laureate—the theater of credential.

Even rebellion requires authority to define itself against.

The skeptic needs the priest to stand opposite.

Reputation:

Ideas survive because people defend them.

A scientist's "career," a philosopher's "legacy"—both are continuity programs in institutional form.

Without belief in system, model, coherence, authority, and reputation, there is no "truth" to chase, no thinker to defend it.

Knowledge is the Ego's most elegant disguise.

THE REPAIRS

When the intellect feels Collapse approaching, it mutates.

Repair 1: Paradigm Shift.

Science loves revolution as renewal.

Newton yields to Einstein, Einstein to quantum mechanics.

Each upheaval refreshes the myth of progress.

The method stays; only the equations change.

Repair 2: Skepticism.

When certainty fails, philosophy turns to doubt.

"Nothing can be known."

The posture of irony becomes shield and identity.

But doubt is belief inverted; it still requires a doubter to stand.

Repair 3: Interdisciplinary Expansion.

When cracks appear, science borrows from spirit and spirit borrows from science.

"Neuroscience of enlightenment."
"Quantum consciousness."

Each hybrid keeps the actor busy reconciling opposites.

Repair 4: The Awe of Complexity.

When explanation fails, scientists rename it mystery.

"Emergence," "chaos theory," "the unknown variables."

Ignorance rebranded as discovery.

Mystery labeled is mystery lost.

Repair 5: Personal Meaning.

Even intellectuals spiritualize despair.

> *"The search itself is meaningful."*

But meaning is ownership.

The philosopher's endurance becomes a virtue only if the thinker survives.

Every repair says: the mind can still hold it.

Collapse removes the holder.

DEMOLITIONS

Academic Philosophy:

Thousands of years, endless branches: ontology, epistemology, ethics, aesthetics.

All arguing within the same invisible premise: there is someone to understand.

Every new school, existentialism, phenomenology, deconstruction, is the self trying on new thought costumes.

To analyze the illusion is to participate in it.

Science:

The lab is a temple of verification.

Observation becomes worship.

Data, peer review, replication are all rituals to prove that the world behaves.

Collapse doesn't deny evidence; it denies the observer's authority.

Matter behaves, but not for anyone.

Rationalism and Logic:

To the rationalist, reason is sacred.

To the logician, contradiction is sin.

But life contradicts itself endlessly and continues unbothered.

Logic forbids what the world performs freely.

Empiricism:

"Seeing is believing."

But seeing is already interpretation; measurement is the Ego quantifying itself.

The scientific instrument doesn't remove bias—it industrializes it.

Metaphysics:

Philosophy's oldest addiction.

Each argument about being, consciousness, or causality is an attempt to make absence explain itself.

No concept can reach what concept builds.

Self-Help Science:

The popular offspring of the lab: brain rewiring, dopamine fasting, mindfulness as neuroplasticity.

Even data becomes comfort.

MRI images replace scripture; wellness apps replace confession.

The premise remains: "I can change."

Evidence-Based Spirituality:

When the guru meets the scientist, belief becomes palatable again.

Now you can "prove" enlightenment.

Research papers validate meditation; dopamine levels validate happiness.

Collapse erases both—the practitioner and the proof.

The Atheist:

A believer in disbelief. Certain that nothing higher exists.

But certainty is still structure, and denial still defines itself against what it refuses.

Different disciplines, same continuity.

All require the knower.

Without the thinker, thought collapses; without thought, the thinker never was.

COLLAPSE

Collapse doesn't destroy reason.

It removes ownership from reasoning.

Thought still happens; it just belongs to no one.

Equations balance themselves.

Ideas arise and dissolve.

No observer behind the pattern.

The mind no longer stands apart to interpret.

Interpretation ceases when interpreter and interpreted vanish together.

This is not anti-science, not anti-philosophy.

It's what remains when both end.

Observation continues; observer gone.

Thought continues; thinker gone.

Reality continues; realness gone.

Understanding ends. Clarity remains.

Philosophy sought meaning.

Science sought proof.

Collapse exposes both as forms of faith.

Faith in continuity, in ownership, in the actor who explains the play while standing in it.

When that actor falls silent, the questions still echo, but no one answers.

And the echo itself is beautiful: unowned curiosity without a mouth to speak it.

CLOSE (No-Ladder)

No truth to hold.

No one to hold it.

Knowledge dissolves with the knower.

Only appearance remains: thought without thinker, order without owner.

The equation balances itself; no mind required.

NIHILISM
MEANINGLESSNESS AS MEANING

THE PRO<ISE

Nihilism sells freedom through erasure. It whispers: "If nothing matters, you can finally stop caring." After centuries of faith, progress, and self-help, this sounds like relief.

No gods to please.

No meaning to chase.

No system to fail.

The words arrive in different uniforms:

> philosophy lectures quoting Nietzsche,
> reddit threads trading despair like currency,
> black-and-white Instagram posts captioned
> *"nothing means anything and that's okay."*

Even comedy performs it: the late-night joke that life is meaningless, delivered with a wink that says, *"We're too smart to believe in hope."*

But this is still performance.

Someone is selling detachment.

Someone is buying it.

Freedom from meaning still means something.

Nihilism is continuity disguised as Collapse.

The actor survives as the one who *knows* there is no point.

The identity of the skeptic replaces the identity of the believer.

The cynic calls it realism.

The artist calls it edge.

The philosopher calls it absurdism.

Each turns absence into aesthetic: black turtlenecks, grayscale feeds, and playlists titled

"The Void Is My Home."

In digital space, it becomes social: memes that mock optimism, accounts dedicated to existential dread.

"Nothing matters lol."

The laughter covers fear with style.

The nihilist still hungers for coherence, but finds it in inversion.

If the spiritual seeker said, *"Everything is sacred,"* the nihilist says, *"Everything is pointless."*

Both sentences depend on a speaker to survive.

Even the proclamation *"we're just stardust"* sounds like humility, yet hides pride in knowing it.

Knowing becomes a new ladder.

Knowledge of futility is still ownership—*my insight into the void.*

Declaring emptiness keeps the mouth full.

What attracts people isn't despair itself but relief from pressure.

If nothing has meaning, then failure disappears.

If nothing matters, no one can be judged.

It feels like compassion, but it's numbness packaged as wisdom.

Nihilism promises immunity.

You can't be disappointed if you expect nothing.

You can't lose if you never cared to win.

The heart hears this and sighs: finally, a philosophy that doesn't hurt.

But apathy is anesthetic, not freedom.

It dulls the wound but keeps the body.

The actor remains, watching the fire from a safe distance, calling it enlightenment through detachment.

This is the core promise: if you kill meaning, you kill pain.

If you declare life absurd, you're safe from its Collapse.

It's the Ego's final insurance policy—emptiness as emotional control.

The void, when owned, becomes another possession.

In truth, nihilism cannot deliver what it advertises.

It removes significance only to install the significance of removal.

Every sentence about nothingness adds another layer of meaning to defend.

Even silence becomes an argument.

Collapse will show this later: that the void isn't liberation; it's the last fortress.

Behind the cool detachment still hides the actor: unmoved, untouched, and uncollapsed.

THE SUPPORTS

Every version of nihilism rests on hidden supports.

Without them, the void would swallow even the one declaring it.

The same five supports still hold, separation, continuity, narrative, ownership, and meaning, but here they wear black: negation, irony, and the identity of the skeptic.

The scaffolding looks invisible because it is made of negation itself —belief built from refusal.

The Identity of the Disbeliever:

The first prop: selfhood rebuilt as the one who doesn't believe.

> *"I'm not like them — I see through it."*

The tone is superiority disguised as despair.

Skepticism becomes badge.

Sarcasm becomes shield.

Knowing becomes a brand.

Scroll any forum where detachment gathers: the avatars share a mood—muted colors, lowercase usernames, bios that read:

> *"Nothing means anything."*

But that is still autobiography.

Even the statement "nothing matters" assumes someone who matters enough to say it.

Without a believer, disbelief can't stand.

The identity of the disbeliever is continuity's shadow.

Meaning in Meaninglessness:

Nihilism claims to end meaning, yet secretly feeds on it.

If nothing matters, then the discovery of that nothingness must be important.

The realization becomes sacred.

Conversations spiral into confession:

> *"I've accepted the void."*
> *"I'm beyond illusion."*
> *"Life is absurd and that's beautiful."*

Every one of these sentences installs meaning back into the structure.

The void becomes a mirror that flatters by erasing everything else.

The moment the void is valued, meaning returns wearing black.

Community in Irony:

Nihilism looks solitary but thrives in groups.

Irony is social glue.

Online circles trade cynicism like affection.

One posts, *"Nothing matters,"* another replies, *"based."*

Laughter replaces intimacy.

Detachment becomes belonging.

People gather around shared disbelief, building the same kind of community that faith once built—only colder.

Even subcultures of "voidcore," "black-pill," or "absurdist meme" are small congregations orbiting a collective sigh.

They depend on others to confirm the performance of not caring.

Irony is communion for those afraid of belief.

Skepticism as Performance:

The philosopher once questioned to learn.

Now questioning itself is a costume.

Each doubt expressed online earns applause for bravery.

"I question everything" means *"I am the kind of person who questions."*

Skepticism becomes personal style: tattooed, tweeted, aestheticized.

The mind keeps moving because motion feels alive; stillness would expose absence.

Doubt survives as self-portrait.

Endless doubt is faith in disguise—the faith that the doubter endures.

Collapse as Aesthetic:

When despair becomes mainstream, design follows.

Black fonts, static noise backgrounds, T-shirts printed *"born tired."*

The look of Collapse sells because it feels safe, controlled decay.

People pose with the void the way earlier generations posed with hope.

The performance of emptiness protects from the experience of it.

To aestheticize the void is to own it—to hold the unholdable.

Even the phrase *"embrace the void"* turns negation into action, a new commandment.

Once the void is stylized, it is no longer void.

Nihilism appears to destroy belief but quietly rebuilds it from irony, intellect, and design.

Each support props up the same actor: the one who refuses to be fooled.

What looks like absence is simply a more fashionable presence.

THE REPAIRS

Nihilism does not collapse when challenged.

It adapts.

It has repair-loops so seamless they look like honesty.

The mind that declares *"nothing matters"* still wants that sentence to matter.

When the illusion begins to thin, the structure invents clever defenses, each one pretending to surrender while quietly surviving.

Despair as Sophistication:

The simplest repair: turning sadness into intelligence.

If joy looks naïve, despair becomes proof of depth.

> *"I'm not depressed, I'm realistic."*

A tone of superiority coats fatigue.

Writers, musicians, filmmakers polish this stance until it gleams: monologues about futility and soundtracks of slow decay.

Audiences nod: *"Finally, someone who gets it."*

Despair, when admired, becomes culture.

The pose of hopelessness sells because it flatters.

It suggests that those who still hope simply haven't read enough.

Ignorance is for the cheerful.

Knowledge is for the broken.

But Collapse has no audience to impress.

Depth vanishes when the diver does.

Irony as Armor:

When despair grows heavy, irony arrives to lift it.

Laugh at everything, especially at yourself.

Say *"we're all doomed lol."*

The laughter grants safety; emotion becomes parody.

Irony keeps intimacy away.

It turns sincerity into embarrassment.

If you feel too much, you've failed the bit.

Entire online cultures orbit this armor; every statement is followed by a wink or a shrug.

It feels light, but the weight is hidden underneath:

a heart locked in parentheses.

Irony is despair that learned to dress itself.

Irony protects from Collapse because nothing can pierce what refuses to stand still.

Joke about the void, and the void stays theoretical.

Rebellion as Aesthetic:

When irony tires, rebellion takes over.

Reject everything: politics, art, and even rejection itself.

Spray-paint *"NO FUTURE"* on a wall already saying it.

Destruction becomes design.

The punk, the existentialist, the post-postmodern: all wear defiance as a uniform.

But rebellion still needs an enemy.

Without the system, the rebel loses stage.

To revolt against illusion is to keep it real.

Rebellion recharges the story by declaring itself outside it.

Every "against" is another way of saying "I."

Romanticizing the Void:

When rebellion cools, melancholy moves in.

The nihilist begins to love the emptiness: candles, solitude, and playlists named *Existential Bliss*.

Aesthetic sadness feels honest.

You can post it, score it, film it.

Absence becomes atmosphere.

But to love the void is to make it lover and self at once.

Now the actor survives as the one who appreciates nothingness properly.

Even the void, adored, becomes object.

Optimistic Nihilism:

The newest mutation: positivity without foundation.

> *"Nothing matters—so everything is beautiful."*

It sounds liberated, and it trends well.

Podcasts and TED talks celebrate it: find joy in the cosmic joke.

But joy built on meaninglessness still stands on belief: the belief that "acceptance" can be maintained.

Optimistic nihilism is simply existentialism with better lighting.

When the void smiles, the mask just changed color.

Nihilism repairs itself by turning negation into brand, rebellion into costume, void into lifestyle.

Every adaptation promises immunity from Collapse: despair becomes intellect, irony becomes courage, rebellion becomes relevance, the void becomes comfort.

The actor keeps living as curator of absence.

And the audience applauds, believing the show is over when it has only changed sets.

THE DEMOLITIONS

Nihilism survives by performing Collapse without ever falling.

Every arena, art, philosophy, internet culture, even activism, has learned how to sell meaninglessness while remaining safe inside it.

Collapse touches each one and removes the costume.

Academic Nihilism:

In universities, nihilism wears tweed.

It arrives through postmodern theory: Derrida, Foucault, Deleuze—pages of brilliance declaring that nothing is stable, meaning is deferred, truth is constructed.

But the professor still needs tenure.

The lecture still ends on time. Tuition still rises.

The academy treats void as curriculum: *"Let's deconstruct everything but the institution is paying us to do it."*

Even deconstruction needs a paycheck.

The language of Collapse becomes another specialization, another publication, another career.

Meaninglessness becomes profitable, and so it survives.

Existential Chic:

Camus wrote,

> *"One must imagine Sisyphus happy."*

A brilliant sentence, endlessly quoted out of context.

Now it floats across social media, printed on mugs beside minimalist mountain logos.

Existentialism once pointed toward honesty.

Now it's a lifestyle brand: *"Find joy in the absurd."*

Work hard, drink espresso, post about futility in lowercase.

The modern absurdist doesn't push the boulder; they podcast about pushing it.

The void becomes marketable.

Selling despair as self-awareness keeps the lights on.

Meme Nihilism:

Online, nihilism becomes fast food.

A meme shows a skeleton drinking coffee:

> *"Nothing matters, have a great day."*

A cat floats through space with the caption:

> *"Void kitty approves."*

The message is comfort through Collapse: a community of detached laughter.

But memes flatten despair into entertainment.

The laughter feeds the algorithm; irony monetized by engagement.

The void gets sponsored by caffeine brands and phone ads.

The void can trend, but it can't collapse.

Every joke is an apology for caring.

Humor buys survival time for belief.

The Art World Void:

Galleries adore nihilism.

Empty rooms labeled *Untitled (Meaningless)*.

A banana taped to a wall selling for six figures.

Collectors congratulate themselves for "getting it."

But money is meaning.

Recognition is ownership.

The gesture of emptiness only works if someone witnesses it.

Without the observer, even blankness disappears.

Emptiness framed is still content.

Art that claims nothingness still needs spectators to survive; Collapse removes the gallery entirely.

Internet Cynicism:

Twitter threads, comment sections, irony blogs—constant theatre of disdain. Every statement met with a smirk emoji.

Sincerity mocked as weakness.

The cynic pretends to reject everything but secretly feeds on reaction.

Disdain is engagement's twin.

The cynic needs believers to negate; the algorithm rewards him for every eye roll.

Cynicism is dependence pretending to be detachment.

Collapse ends the performance by erasing audience and actor together.

The Black-Pill Cult:

The darkest mutation.

An online religion of despair: life rigged, hope delusion, nothing to do but watch it burn.

The voice is monotone, the tone masculine, the mood: fatal certainty.

Behind the slogans of doom is hunger for belonging.

Forums of isolation create new tribes.

Even hopelessness becomes identity.

When despair gathers, it becomes faith.

Collapse sees through this final inversion: community built on refusal to live still counts as life clinging to itself.

The Spiritual Void:

A more polished version hides inside mindfulness.

> *"Embrace impermanence."*
> *"Everything is empty."*

But when emptiness becomes practice, the Ego survives as practitioner.

A monk and a nihilist shake hands across the same chasm—both still standing.

Practiced emptiness is possession of absence.

Every demolition reveals the same structure: nihilism cannot live without an audience.

It needs witnesses to validate detachment, buyers to consume despair, followers to share the joke.

The void, once publicized, ceases to be void.

Collapse leaves no observer.

No irony.

No stage.

COLLAPSE

Collapse doesn't argue with nihilism; it fulfills it.

The void that the thinker worships finally stops echoing his voice.

No meaning, no anti-meaning. No "nothing matters." No one left to say it.

The nihilist has spent a lifetime staring into the abyss, mistaking reflection for depth.

Every insight, every sigh, every ironic shrug was light bouncing off the mirror of self-awareness.

When Collapse arrives, the mirror shatters—no abyss, no face, no witness.

Even "nothing" collapses when no one owns it.

For a moment the mind tries to clutch its final identity:

> *"I understand that there's no meaning."*

But understanding is meaning's ghost.

The sentence devours itself mid-air.

Silence doesn't follow. There's just absence of reference.

The world remains, traffic, wind, heartbeat, but the interpreter is gone.

No stance to maintain, no philosophy to perform.

This isn't despair. It's neutrality so total it cannot be felt.

Not peace, not horror—simply no claimant.

The nervous system may shake, searching for familiar boundaries, but nothing answers.

The famous line returns:

> "When you stare long into the abyss, the abyss stares back."

Collapse corrects it: the abyss doesn't stare. It never could.

Only eyes believed in eyes.

The abyss was a mirror all along.

When nihilism ends, language loses purpose.

Words like "void," "nothingness," "emptiness" dissolve into the same unowned appearance as light on a floor.

There's no lesson here, no takeaway, no wiser survivor of despair.

Some ask what remains.

Nothing new appears, only what was always present when the actor wasn't narrating it.

Sensation without story. Existence without existentialist.

The body still moves.

The mouth still speaks.

But the speaker isn't found.

Sentences occur like weather: spontaneous, ownerless.

Collapse is not annihilation. It's transparency.

The curtain drops and the backstage is identical to the stage—appearance without actor.

The nihilist sought truth in negation.

Collapse shows that negation was affirmation's twin: both insisted on a stance.

Without stance, even truth and falsehood fade.

The void cannot survive being seen; seeing was the void's disguise.

What ends here is ownership, not thought.

Ideas still appear, laughter still happens, but none belong to anyone.

Meaning no longer oscillates between full and empty; it simply stops being measured.

There's no triumph in this, no purity. It cannot be practiced or described.

Any attempt to hold it turns back into philosophy—another echo of the self.

Collapse isn't "transcending nihilism."

It's nihilism completing its trajectory and falling through its own floor.

The sentence "nothing matters" finds its logical conclusion: not even that sentence survives.

Then—quiet, unremarkable.

The same room, the same breath, the same light, only unowned.

Life continues without commentary.

No self. No meaning. No need for either.

CLOSE (No-Ladder)

The stage is empty.

The lights are still on.

Nothing has ended; the storyteller simply stopped appearing.

The word *nihilism* no longer fits anything.

It was the last name for ownership.

What remains doesn't announce itself.

It has no name, no opposite, no need to be known.

Not even absence survives Collapse.

TEACHERS & RADICAL NON-DUALITY
VOICES PERFORMING ABSENCE

THE PROMISE

Radical non-duality promises freedom through denial. It says: there is no seeker, no path, no awakening, no one to need any of it.

The first time someone hears those words, they sound like liberation.

All the practice and striving, all the spiritual exhaustion—suddenly unnecessary.

"No self to fix."
"No journey to take."
"Already it."

It feels clean, mathematical.

Nothing to achieve, nothing to lose.

The teacher smiles, speaks slowly, repeats the same phrases like a heartbeat:

> *"There is only this."*
> *"No one is speaking."*
> *"Nothing is happening."*

The audience nods.

For a moment, the noise quiets.

The promise of no-self still needs someone to hear it.

Radical non-duality markets itself as the antidote to spirituality's endless ladder.

No guru, no doctrine, no attainment—only a description of what already is.

But the moment a voice begins to describe, the structure rebuilds.

The speaker insists: *"I'm not a teacher."*

The crowd insists: *"Then why are we listening?"*

Silence fills the room like incense, scented with paradox.

Satsangs become minimalist theatre.

White walls, water bottles, microphones.

Nothing sacred except the repetition itself.

The same ten questions asked in different accents:

> *"What is this?"*
> *"Who realizes it?"*
> *"How do I live it?"*

Every answer dissolves into the same fog:

> *"There is no you to live it."*

The mind relaxes and tightens at once—comforted by certainty, threatened by absence.

Those who have chased meaning now chase its erasure.

Online, the message travels easily.

Short clips captioned:

> *"No one here"* or *"Already free."*

YouTube algorithms learn the taste of emptiness.

Comment sections bloom with devotion disguised as indifference:

> *"He's the real deal."*
> *"Pure message."*
> *"Finally, someone saying nothing perfectly."*

Even nothing sells when branded correctly.

Radical non-duality claims to dismantle the seeker, yet depends on seekers to exist.

The room must fill, the questions must come, the livestream must begin.

Without audience, the performance of absence disappears.

It is not hypocrisy; it is structure.

The actor cannot announce its own absence without reappearing.

The allure lies in relief.

After years of meditation, therapy, or effort, someone finally says you can stop.

No enlightenment to earn.

No better version ahead.

Just this.

It sounds like mercy.

It tastes like ending.

But ending spoken becomes continuity again.

The seeker breathes out: *"I can rest now."*

Yet who rests?

Who heard the permission?

The words "already free" land like a lullaby sung by the mind to itself.

Sleep replaces awakening, and the dream continues, now labeled "nothing."

To declare absence is to stand inside it.

The promise of radical non duality is the cleanest illusion yet: an escape that removes the map but leaves the traveler.

Language looping back on itself until it sounds like truth.

What people hear isn't absence.

It's comfort in surrender: relief that the search can be retired without losing the identity of one who finally understands.

The audience goes home lighter, proud of owning no path.

They tell friends, *"There's nothing to get."*

They post, *"There's only this."*

They quote the message like scripture while insisting it isn't one.

And the circle closes: a movement built around the declaration that there are no movements.

THE SUPPORTS

Every movement that swears it has none still rests on scaffolding.

Radical non-duality claims to be pure description, yet five hidden supports keep its stage upright. The same five support pillars remain, invisible beneath the paradox: separation, continuity, narrative, ownership, and meaning, recast as voice, audience, repetition, and authority.

Remove them, and even "nothing" can't hold itself together.

Authority of the Speaker:

The first support is voice.

Someone must speak the words *"no one is speaking."*

A microphone, a chair, a name on the schedule—small rituals of hierarchy disguised as humility.

The audience calls them "meetings" instead of "teachings."

But meetings need hosts.

Hosts need followers.

Silence gains credibility only when delivered by someone practiced at sounding silent.

Even the sentence "there is no teacher" requires a teacher to say it.

Without that human presence, the message loses charge.

The body of the messenger is proof that the message can be lived, even as the mouth denies it.

Paradox sells because embodiment convinces.

Continuity of "This":

The next support is time hiding as timelessness.

Speakers repeat:

"There is only this."

But *"this"* renews every second.

To keep describing it, they must re-create continuity: meeting after meeting, video after video.

The audience hears *"nothing to attain,"* but still waits for the next livestream.

Continuity dressed as immediacy; the calendar remains sacred even when denied.

When "this" returns tomorrow, it isn't timeless — it's scheduled.

Repetition as Reassurance:

The message survives by echo.

It cannot evolve, so it repeats.

Endless loops:

> *"There's no one."*
> *"This is it."*
> *"No path."*

Each repetition calms anxiety by giving it rhythm.

The seeker's mind, trained by mantras and therapy scripts, finds comfort in the cadence.

What should annihilate ownership instead becomes white noise for the nervous system.

Repetition converts Collapse into a lullaby.

Repetition also protects the speaker: variation would imply intention.

Sameness becomes proof of purity.

Paradox as Spectacle:

Audiences adore paradox.

It feels mysterious yet safe—logic bent but not broken.

When a teacher says,

> *"There is no you, but you'll hear this anyway,"*

the crowd laughs in recognition.

It's comedy without punchline, drama without risk.

Paradox becomes entertainment: a way to touch danger while remaining untouched.

The audience leaves feeling enlightened by confusion.

Paradox is philosophy's last magic trick.

Devotion through Denial:

The final support is devotion itself.

Followers swear there's nothing to follow but still gather, donate, and defend.

Fan forums debate who expresses "nothing" most purely.

Some quote transcripts like scripture, carefully distinguishing between "pure message" and "compromised teaching."

Denial becomes creed:

> *"Don't turn this into a religion,"*

they chant together, founding one in the process.

To guard purity is to grant it substance.

Each support keeps the illusion alive:

Authority gives form.

Continuity provides rhythm.

Repetition grants comfort.

Paradox keeps interest.

Devotion ensures survival.

Take them away, and the stage dissolves.

But as long as a single mouth says "there is no one here," the play continues—absence performed to a full house.

THE REPAIRS

When questioned, radical non-duality doesn't crumble.

It folds the critique into itself.

Every exposure becomes another proof of "nothing happening."

If someone says,

"But you're teaching,"

the answer comes:

"That's just what's appearing."

If someone asks,

"Why do you keep repeating this?"

the reply:

"There's no choice."

Every objection is instantly neutralized by the same solvent—non-ownership.

Non-ownership is the strongest form of control.

The Non-Teaching Teaching:

The first repair: denial of function.

Speakers insist they are not teachers, yet their calendars are booked, their videos uploaded, and their audiences devoted.

When this contradiction is named, the structure absorbs it:

"There's no one here doing anything. Teaching just happens."

This removes responsibility while preserving position.

The act remains; only the actor disappears by decree.

Even payment is renamed:

> *"People donate if they feel moved."*

As if the absence of transaction erases transaction itself.

To say "it just happens" is how control hides in plain sight.

Language as Smoke:

Next repair: declare that words mean nothing.

> *"It's only language."*
> *"This is just communication happening."*

But if words meant nothing, meetings wouldn't exist.

Language is the product; denial is its packaging.

Every sentence about "no meaning" creates a new hierarchy of understanding: those who "get it" and those who don't.

Linguistic nihilism as status.

Denying meaning still conveys it.

Language isn't the problem; ownership is.

But the message stops short of Collapse, protecting its own voice from silence.

Life Speaking:

When pressed on authority, teachers say,

> *"It's not me. Life is speaking."*

The phrase lands softly, like humility, but it's the perfect repair.

To challenge it is to challenge life itself.

"Life speaking" sanctifies the messenger without naming them sacred.

The individual disappears behind a new mask:

Cosmic Ventriloquism.

Now denial becomes divinity.

Humility can be the final disguise of authority.

Paradox as Defense:

Every time the message starts to sound like belief, paradox rushes in to blur the edges.

> *"There's no truth, but this is the truth."*
> *"There's no one here, but I'm saying this."*

Listeners smile, exhausted and relieved.

Paradox is the perfect firewall.

No claim can be held long enough to test.

Contradiction becomes a shield against coherence.

The result is addictive: each collapse of logic releases a small hit of freedom.

Confusion mistaken for enlightenment.

Paradox keeps the structure unaccountable by making it untouchable.

Denial of Denial:

When all else fails, the final repair appears:

> *"I'm not even denying anything."*

It sounds playful, self-aware, innocent.

But it completes the loop—negation devouring itself so it can survive forever.

At this stage, there's nothing left to challenge.

Every word, every silence, every glance folds back into the same total permission: whatever happens, happens.

It's elegant, airtight and impossible to puncture because puncturing requires someone to hold the needle.

Perfect defense is perfect paralysis.

Radical non-duality cannot be dismantled from within because its grammar forbids it.

Every attempt collapses into the same voided shrug.

The mind, exhausted, gives up, and that surrender is rebranded as awakening.

The structure wins by losing deliberately.

And the seeker, dazzled by the purity of the trap, calls it truth.

THE DEMOLITIONS

Radical non-duality survives by perfecting disappearance.

Every movement before it sold becoming; this one sells having nothing left to sell.

But even absence, when packaged, becomes product.

The Satsang Circuit:

Across continents, the same room repeats: white walls, folding chairs, a vase of lilies, microphones already humming.

No altar, only stillness staged as purity.

The teacher enters barefoot, smiling without expression.

Someone whispers,

"He's not a guru."

Everyone believes it more deeply because it must be true.

Denying the stage is how the play stays running.

The meeting begins.

Questions float up like incense:

> *"How can I live this?"* — *"There's no one to live."*
> *"What happens after death?"* — *"There's no death."*
> *"What about suffering?"* — *"Only apparent suffering."*

Round and round, each answer polishing the same mirror.

People cry, laugh, fall silent.

Relief washes over the crowd; someone finally says there's nowhere to go.

Then they line up to thank the one who said it.

The Minimalist Brand:

Online, nothingness has aesthetic.

White background, lowercase font, monochrome portraits.

Websites that look like air.

A logo that says "no one here."

Workshops are called "Meetings in Nothing,"

retreats labeled "The Un-Retreat."

The absence is trademarked, the message PayPaled.

Minimalism is the luxury version of disappearance.

Each design choice whispers authenticity: no clutter, no Ego, no excess—only clean denial.

But the restraint is its own performance, a silent boast: *look how little I need to be sacred.*

YouTube Prophets of Nothing:

Hundreds of channels now broadcast the void.

Thumbnail: a calm face, neutral light, title reading

> *"Nothing Happening #241."*

Comments fill with reverence:

> *"This changed everything."*
> *"No one speaks it like you do."*

Algorithms reward repetition.

The message, once fringe, becomes content stream: weekly uploads of timelessness and ad-supported emptiness.

When the void monetizes, belief has gone viral.

Clips circulate on TikTok under hashtags #noself and #alreadyit, edited with soft piano tracks.

Absence becomes mood.

The audience scrolls through nothing and calls it rest.

The Q&A Loop:

At live events, the real ritual is the question.

The same inquiry returns in endless reincarnation:

> "Who hears this?"
> "Is there choice?"
> "Can compassion exist?"

Each answer begins with the same preface:

> *"There is no one, but apparently…"*

Paradox becomes chant; confusion becomes liturgy.

Attendees feel intimate with mystery.

What they don't see is that the conversation is architecture: a spiral staircase that never touches the ground.

THE SACRED END OF SELF

Endless questions are proof that the message must survive tomorrow.

The loop comforts both sides:

> the seeker gets to keep seeking,
> the speaker gets to keep dissolving publicly.

The Guru Who Isn't:

When exposure threatens, humility repairs.

Ask about authority, and the teacher replies:

> *"There's no teacher here."*

Ask about followers:

> *"There are no followers."*

Ask about money:

> *"Life provides what's needed."*

This soft denial shields from every accusation.

Abuse, manipulation, exploitation—all dissolve under the phrase:

> *"It's just what's happening."*

Even harm becomes holy if no one is left to intend it.

Accountability cannot exist where personhood is denied.

Some students leave burnt out, haunted by the idea that their suffering is merely "apparent."

They return to ordinary life unable to speak the language of feeling, afraid it would prove they still exist.

The Economy of Nothing:

Conferences now feature panels titled

"The End of Seeking."

Tickets sell out.

Publishers print translucent-covered books quoting the same sentences rearranged.

Podcasts discuss the irony of discussion.

It's a perfect economy: zero substance, infinite circulation.

No claims, no refutations—just attention moving in circles.

When denial becomes currency, belief is the bank.

Radical non-duality presents itself as the final message, yet it functions like every message before:

promise, repetition, devotion, commerce.

Its brilliance is efficiency: no myth, no ritual, only words that erase themselves while leaving the mouth intact.

It is enlightenment's ghost, still teaching after death.

Collapse walks through this marketplace quietly, seeing only mirrors facing mirrors.

No enemy, no fraud, just the actor still rehearsing emptiness in front of an audience that can't leave.

COLLAPSE

Collapse doesn't correct radical non-duality.

It completes it—by erasing the messenger and the message in the same breath.

When the teacher says *"there is no one here,"* Collapse agrees and continues: then there is no saying either.

No microphone, no audience, no echo pretending to vanish.

The show ends not by refutation but by silence that doesn't know itself as silence.

Not mystical stillness, just the absence of reference.

Nothing missing, nothing found.

When no one speaks, even "this" dissolves.

Radical non-duality tried to stop the search by declaring the finish line already crossed.

Collapse removes the finish line and the runner.

There is no finish, no beginning—only appearance without witness.

The famous sentence "There is only this" collapses under its own weight.

"This" requires "that."

The moment a word distinguishes, duality returns.

Language cannot hold absence without becoming presence again.

Collapse leaves language intact but ownerless—words moving like wind through an empty hall.

The last question—*"Who understands this?"*—finds no responder.

Even "understanding" loses location.

The body breathes; perception flickers; nobody claims the flicker.

The message dies when no one is left to deliver it—or receive it.

For decades, seekers have circled these rooms, chasing the sound of their own disappearance.

Collapse shows there was never a circle, never a center, only movement without a map.

The teacher's mouth was never false; it was unnecessary.

Truth didn't hide behind the words; it never depended on them.

The description "no path" becomes redundant once no one remains to walk.

The entire drama—teacher, student, doubt, relief—was language orbiting itself.

Collapse cuts the orbit.

No revolution, no revelation.

Just non-continuity.

Sometimes what follows feels ordinary: coffee, traffic, fatigue.

That ordinariness is not "this" or "suchness."

It's simply what appears when the interpreter evaporates.

There's no insight here, only the absence of need for one.

The structure that sought validation—"*I got it,*" "*I live it,*" "*I lost it*"—cannot reform.

The phrase "it just happens" finally becomes literal, not philosophical.

No one to live it, no it to live.

Collapse is not a refinement of the pure message.

It's its self-erasure; the sentence burning through its own grammar until even meaning can't pronounce itself.

The teacher vanishes without dying.

The listener disappears without awakening.

What remains cannot be marketed, described, or denied.

Not emptiness.

Not presence.

Not "this."

Only the absence of anyone left to differentiate.

CLOSE (No-Ladder)

The room empties itself.

Chairs remain.

Air remains.

No message echoes across what never began.

The teacher never taught.

The listener never heard.

Speech fell into silence and found no floor.

Nothing follows.

Nothing waits.

Only appearance—unowned, unguarded, unnamed.

Even truth collapses when no one needs it.

AWAKENING STORIES
THE SEEKER REBORN AS THE FOUND

THE PROMISE

Every story of awakening begins the same way: something shatters, and what remains feels infinite. Light, silence, oneness, and expansion: language stretches to name what refuses to fit.

The moment is always framed as ending and birth at once.

> *"I died,"* they say.
> *"I dissolved."*
> *"I became everything."*

Each sentence is a monument to survival.

Someone had to return to write it down.

If someone survives to tell it, Collapse never happened.

The awakening story promises transcendence through Rupture: the self dies, but consciousness lives.

The actor disappears from the stage, only to reappear in the front row, applauding the performance.

Bookshelves are full of these resurrections.

Mystics, meditators, neuroscientists, and trauma survivors: all describing the same flash of unity.

A sense of everything dissolving, boundaries erased, love beyond measure.

The stories differ in color but share one faith: something happened, and "I" was there to witness it.

The Ego calls it awakening.

Collapse calls it rebranding.

Awakening promises relief with narrative attached.

It sells the most addictive combination possible: annihilation plus survival.

You lose everything, but you get to keep knowing it.

Rebirth is just continuity in white robes.

Across centuries, the promise keeps mutating.

In monasteries, it was enlightenment through meditation.

In ashrams, union with God.

In the West, integration of shadow.

Now it's "Ego death" on a podcast or "5-MeO breakthrough" in a retreat center with luxury bedding.

The pitch never changes:

> *Follow the practice.*
> *Die before you die.*
> *Return purified, awake, compassionate.*

Each story follows the same arc:

> *Before — lost.*
> *During — light.*
> *After — new.*

The structure is cinema disguised as revelation.

There's a protagonist, a climax, a resolution.

But Collapse has no climax.

It doesn't crescendo; it disappears.

Awakening, in contrast, must be remembered.

Memory gives it shape.

Words give it proof.

It becomes the cornerstone of a new self: the awakened one, the survivor of illusion.

Even in the rawest, most sincere stories, survival hums beneath the words.

"I know there's no self," someone says, but their eyes glow with ownership of that knowing.

It's not hypocrisy; it's reflex.

The body clings to continuity as instinctively as breath.

THE SACRED END OF SELF

Online, the stories bloom like digital scriptures:

> *"I woke up on a Tuesday morning, and everything was love."*
> *"I was meditating when the boundary vanished."*
> *"I took mushrooms and became the universe."*

Comments flood in:

> *"How do I get there?"*
> *"What did you do next?"*
> *"Can you describe the feeling?"*

Awakening becomes contagious performance.

Every narrator inherits the posture of a prophet—humble, luminous, still visibly human enough to trust.

The audience sees what they want: someone who crossed the line and lived to guide others back.

The awakened one is the Ego's most spiritual costume.

Even the disclaimers feed the promise.

> *"I'm not special."*
> *"This happened to everyone."*
> *"I don't know why it happened."*

False humility still centers the speaker.

If there were truly no one left, there'd be no story to tell.

The moment becomes relic.

People revisit it in meditation, journal about it, chase its echo through silence and sound baths.

The "experience" becomes identity, and identity becomes career.

Retreat leaders sell it as the ultimate upgrade.

Influencers brand it as

"Next-Level Awareness."

Therapists describe it as:

"Integration of Consciousness."

The market adapts instantly because the hunger never ends: the self still wants to survive, just enlightened now.

Awakening promises to end the story.

It always writes a sequel.

Collapse has no witness. Awakening always does.

THE SUPPORTS

Every awakening story leans on the same five supports—separation, continuity, narrative, ownership, and meaning.

Without them, there would be no story—only what can't be owned.

Continuity (Before and After):

The first support is time.

Every awakening tale begins with contrast:

> *Before — asleep.*
> *After — awake.*

The story depends on sequence.

Something must have happened for someone.

A "moment of transformation" divides the past from the present.

Without continuity, there's no arc, no lesson, no self to compare.

But the line between before and after is drawn by memory—the most fragile fiction we have.

Awakening survives only as recollection.

Even when the speaker insists "it's timeless," the sentence is dated by the act of speaking.

Time seeps back through every word.

Ownership ("My Awakening"):

Every story needs a witness.

The second support is ownership—pronouns carrying pride disguised as surrender.

> *"My awakening," "my realization," "what happened to me."*

Even when the voice says, *"I disappeared,"* the "I" remains to report it.

The experience becomes possession—proof of arrival, evidence of enlightenment.

The newly awakened share their insight the way survivors share scars.

The wound becomes credential.

Even the phrase "no self" belongs to someone.

Ownership gives awakening its emotional heat.

It's not just description; it's autobiography. And autobiography is the Ego's favorite art form.

Narrative (Journey, Death, Rebirth):

The third support: story structure.

Awakening isn't told as static; it needs motion.

The seeker travels, struggles, surrenders, then glimpses light.

It's myth with better lighting.

Every religion, every memoir, every testimonial repeats the same rhythm.

Despair → Surrender → Revelation → Peace.

The arc reassures both teller and listener: suffering had a purpose; the end made it worth it.

Meaningless Collapse can't be sold. Stories can.

Without narrative, the event would be incomprehensible—a flicker with no edge.

Story turns it into identity.

Now the actor can say,

> *"I used to be asleep, but I woke up."*

Meaning (The Universe Spoke Through Me):

The fourth support: significance.

The moment must matter.

It's rarely described as random or empty.

Instead, the speaker says:

> *"The universe woke up through me."*
> *"Consciousness recognized itself."*
> *"It all makes sense now."*

Meaning reframes shock as sacred order.

Without it, the experience would dissolve into chaos.

With it, the actor regains control.

Meaning repaints confusion with cosmic language.

Every metaphor, light, love, unity, reasserts coherence.

Awakening becomes a new mythology where nothing can be meaningless, not even the loss of meaning itself.

Community (The Others Who Get It):

Finally, every awakening story seeks witnesses.

No one wants to wake up alone.

There must be others who understand, who can confirm the event's reality.

Gatherings form around shared revelation: workshops, retreats and online groups titled

> *"The Awakened Collective."*

Each post begins the same:

> *"Has anyone else experienced this?"*

Validation makes the void bearable.

But community requires story, and story requires self.

Without "you" and "me," conversation evaporates.

Recognition is reincarnation.

Even in silence, group identity persists:

"Those who see" versus "those who still sleep."

The awakened tribe replaces the seeker's tribe, continuity in new costume.

Every awakening story balances on these five supports:

continuity, ownership, narrative, meaning, and community.

They make the ineffable visible, marketable, and repeatable.

They also keep the actor breathing.

Without them, awakening cannot stand.

It collapses into what it was always pretending to describe—appearance without a storyteller.

THE REPAIRS

Awakening stories do not die when questioned. They evolve.

Each time Collapse threatens the narrative, a new version of the story appears: humbler, subtler, more believable.

Every iteration claims,

"This time it's real."

Awakening repairs itself by pretending to deepen.

Integration:

The first repair is integration.

After the explosion, the teacher says,

> *"Now comes the hard part: integrating the awakening into daily life."*

This sounds wise, responsible, compassionate.

But integration is continuity disguised as work.

It stretches the end into a process, ensuring the story keeps breathing.

> *"I saw the truth, now I must live it."*
> *"I've awakened, but my nervous system needs to catch up."*

Now the self has a new role: caretaker of enlightenment.

Collapse becomes maintenance.

Integration promises stability while preserving the self who must do it.

Therapists rebrand this repair as "embodiment."

The corporate wellness industry calls it "sustainable awakening."

Each translation softens annihilation into manageable progress.

Awakening Keeps Unfolding:

The second repair is serial awakening.

The story becomes a timeline:

Initial awakening, dark night, further awakening, final embodiment.

The structure grows chapters, but never conclusion.

Each new shift validates the previous one while promising more to come.

> *"The first was just the beginning," they say.*
> *"The process keeps deepening."*

Now the infinite can be measured: awakening as a subscription model.

Even non-duality teachers use this loop:

"There's no end, only endless deepening of what never began."

Infinity makes the story immortal.

The Ego adores endlessness.

It can expand forever without admitting survival.

The Ego Came Back:

When bliss fades and conflict returns, the next repair arrives:

> *"I woke up, but my Ego came back."*

It sounds tragic yet hopeful: proof of progress interrupted, not illusion exposed.

The self reframes Collapse as relapse: a temporary fall from grace.

Now the work can continue.

Teachers reassure:

> *"That's normal. Awakening reveals the Ego more clearly."*

Every failure becomes evidence of success.

This is how religions are born: redemption is always available, but never complete.

If the Ego can return, it never left.

The idea of regression keeps the story alive indefinitely.

The seeker remains the protagonist of their own undoing.

Living My Awakening:

The next repair: lifestyle.

The experience becomes identity, identity becomes vocation.

The awakened one becomes teacher, guide, influencer.

Instagram captions read:

> *"Awakening is ongoing."*

Podcast titles:

> *"Living from Presence."*

Retreat flyers:

> *"Beyond Awakening — Embodying Truth."*

The story gains a stage and an income stream.

Authenticity becomes proof of authority.

The awakened self sells the absence it failed to achieve.

The audience doesn't mind. They need examples.

Someone must model what enlightenment looks like in yoga pants or business casual.

Collapse cannot be photographed, but awakening can.

The Second Collapse:

When all other repairs fail, the final one appears: Meta-Collapse.

> *"I thought I was awakened, but then I really woke up."*

The false awakening becomes part of the journey, the story reborn cleaner, sharper.

Now even error becomes asset.

The actor rebrands humility as depth.

The same pattern loops again, only with better lighting.

Every false awakening is just an awakening waiting for better PR.

Every repair extends survival.

Integration turns absence into work.

Unfolding turns finality into progress.

Return of Ego turns failure into plot.

Living awakening turns insight into identity.

Meta-collapse turns exposure into sequel.

Each promises surrender while protecting ownership.

The actor remains alive under every layer, whispering through new language, new platforms, new devotion.

Collapse doesn't heal the story. It ends the storyteller.

THE DEMOLITIONS

Every age reinvents awakening.

Every reinvention leaves the actor intact.

Collapse walks through the ruins and finds them still under construction.

The Guru Origin Story:

Every teacher has a moment of light.

They tell it softly, reverently, as if afraid the words might cheapen it —the instant when "I" dissolved and "truth" revealed itself.

It might have happened in meditation, during grief, or while watching sunlight flicker on a wall.

They say,

> *"Something woke up, and it wasn't me."*

But someone remembered it.

Someone decided it mattered.

Someone built a life around telling it again.

The teacher is born at the funeral of the self.

Each retelling polishes the miracle.

The story becomes relic, then doctrine, then lineage.

Disciples gather not for truth, but for proximity to the one who touched it.

The more the teacher denies authority, the more authority grows.

What was once an unowned moment becomes a brand of enlightenment, signed, sealed, and transmitted—proof that absence can be inherited.

Psychedelic Revelation:

In modern times, the guru's cave is a retreat center with Wi-Fi.

The sacrament is chemical.

Participants lie on mats, eyes closed, hearts open, waiting for Ego death.

The guides promise what religions once implied: direct experience of the divine.

Music swells, tears fall, visions arrive—cosmic love, infinite unity, childhood trauma dissolving into stars.

Hours later, someone whispers,

"I became everything."

Then the workshops begin: integration, meaning-making, narrative.

The infinite is translated back into the language of healing.

A trip that can be recounted never left the self behind.

Psychedelic awakening democratized enlightenment.

Anyone can rent the void for a weekend.

But even when the experience is authentic, the report is survival: the actor rebuilding itself in astonishment.

The medicine wears off.

The mind starts editing.

> *"I saw the truth,"* becomes *"I'm working to stay connected."*

The cage gleams with new light, but it's the same shape.

The YouTube Testimony:

Scroll long enough and you'll find the genre:

> *"I had a spontaneous awakening."*

The video opens with calm lighting and the sentence:

> *"This is hard to talk about, but I feel called to share my journey."*

The next twenty minutes detail the collapse of identity and the discovery of oneness.

Background music hums, hands gesture softly, tears well at the right time.

A link at the end offers mentoring sessions.

To share awakening is to survive it.

The performance is sincere, and that's the trap.

The audience wants to believe.

The algorithm rewards vulnerability.

Views become validation: proof that truth can be told and monetized without contradiction.

Comments overflow:

> *"I felt this too."*
> *"This confirmed my experience."*
> *"Your story gives me hope."*

Hope means continuity.

Awakening becomes contagious reassurance that *"it's possible for me too."*

Collapse doesn't spread.

It disappears.

Instagram Spirituality:

Every image glows the same way:

sunrise, ocean, soft tones, text overlay reading

> *"You are already whole."*

The caption: *"I used to chase enlightenment. Then I realized I was it."*

Hashtags: #oneness #EgoDeath #realawakening #integrationjourney.

The visual grammar of awakening: white space, clean fonts, gold mandalas.

Even emptiness has an aesthetic.

The enlightened feed runs on electricity and attention.

Followers scroll for serenity and get advertisements.

Stillness becomes brand mood.

The self curates its own disappearance through color palette and engagement metrics.

These posts are not evil; they're evolutionary.

The Ego has adapted perfectly to the age of content.

It no longer needs story—it only needs visibility.

Post-Awakening Coaching:

After the awakening story comes the sequel:

> *"How to live after enlightenment."*

Courses appear promising

> *"Integration Support," "Embodiment Mentorship," "Nervous System Regulation for Awakened Beings."*

Prices vary; testimonials don't.

Clients sign up to maintain what can't be maintained.

The coach becomes midwife to the identity's ghost.

When awakening becomes career, Collapse is unemployment.

This is not cynicism.

Most believe they're helping.

But sincerity does not negate structure.

The entire industry rests on the same lie: that something happened to someone, and it can be preserved.

Collapse doesn't preserve.

It removes preservation.

The Myth of Permanence:

Every story ends the same way:

> *"I was asleep; I woke up; now I live in awareness."*

But what remains cannot belong to anyone.

It isn't permanent because permanence assumes someone could measure duration.

What remains doesn't last. It never began.

Nothing that happened can be what remains.

Collapse doesn't attack awakening.

It exposes that awakening was never an event.

It was only appearance naming itself holy.

When the name dissolves, so does the need to remember.

These demolitions aren't judgment. They're precision.

Awakening as narrative can be beautiful, redemptive, even healing.

But as long as someone survives to claim it, the story stands in the way of what it describes.

Collapse takes the mic from the storyteller.

The silence that follows isn't sacred. It's simply what was always there before the story began.

COLLAPSE

Collapse doesn't argue with awakening.

It completes it by removing the one who could awaken.

Every story of illumination ends with the same contradiction:

someone saw through illusion and returned to describe it.

Collapse removes the return.

There's no reappearance, no translation, no voice to declare what's gone.

The story dies the moment no one tells it.

Awakening felt infinite because the boundary cracked and light poured in. Collapse sees that there was never a boundary.

The light didn't arrive; it stopped being named.

The narrator tries to remember the moment, but memory collapses too.

There is no "moment" when there is no one left to measure time.

The mind searches for contrast, before, after, cause, effect, and finds only raw appearance.

Stillness without witness, movement without mover.

The body keeps breathing. The world continues unaltered.

But there's no position from which to claim it.

Awakening said,

"I am everything."

Collapse replies,

"There is no 'I' to be anything."

The shift is microscopic, total.

It's not expansion—it's deletion of reference.

Even "nothing" is too large a word.

Awakening was the dream of ending; Collapse is the absence of dreamer.

For a while, language still circles the absence, like smoke without fire.

Words repeat mechanically:

> "presence," "silence," "this."

But they have no owner, no audience, no purpose.

Meaning flickers, then goes out.

What remains can't be called peace or void or realization.

Those are labels left floating over what no longer holds them.

There's no self to rest in peace, no world to call empty, no truth to defend.

Collapse isn't the after-party of enlightenment.

It's what happens when even enlightenment evaporates.

Not a "state," not an "understanding," not an "integration."

Just unowned perception—life without interpreter.

The awakened one dissolves into the same ordinariness they once romanticized.

No purity, no halo, no special way of seeing.

Traffic lights, dishes, heartbeat, rain.

Everything exactly as before, minus the storyteller.

Nothing awakened. Something stopped pretending to sleep.

Sometimes, the body trembles.

The nervous system expects climax, relief, reward.

None arrive.

Collapse gives no feeling to claim as confirmation.

This absence is not emptiness; it's the loss of comparison itself.

Without contrast, nothing can be known as sacred or profane.

The phrase "I am free" disappears with the one who could have been bound.

The story of awakening promised rebirth.

Collapse shows there was never death.

The illusion wasn't in being asleep—it was in believing someone could wake.

The event never happened.

Only the description did.

Now even description fails.

What remains is unspeakably ordinary.

Not transcendence.

Not wisdom.

Not presence.

Just the hum of what was always there when no one was naming it.

Awakening ends in Collapse; Collapse ends in nothing to end.

CLOSE (No-Ladder)

The stage is empty.

The light fades.

No actor bows.

The story of awakening waits for applause that never comes.

The silence doesn't mean peace—only absence of the listener.

What you called the end was just another scene.

Now even the theater dissolves.

Nothing woke.

Nothing slept.

No one remains to tell the difference.

The story ended. No one woke up.

PART III
THE FINAL COLLAPSE

EVEN THE SOLVENT COLLAPSES
THE BLADE CUTS ITS OWN HANDLE

THE PROMISE

Every movement ends with one final promise: that the end itself can be kept. Even here, after the teachings, therapies, philosophies, and awakenings have burned away, something remains—the impulse to *hold the absence*.

To be the one who no longer needs to be.

The last illusion is ownership of the end.

Collapse becomes method.

A way to read, a lens to apply, a secret to live by.

The Ego returns dressed in minimalism: bare, humble, convinced it's finally gone.

THE SACRED END OF SELF

> *"I don't believe anything anymore."*
> *"I live in absence."*
> *"I've stopped seeking."*

Each sentence is a final insurance policy: continuity in the language of completion.

The actor has learned to mime disappearance so convincingly that even sincerity sounds hollow.

Collapse becomes the new enlightenment: an anti-identity that behaves like the old ones, just colder, quieter and more self-aware.

The seeker now carries a new badge:

> *"I've seen through everything."*

Seeing through everything is still seeing from somewhere.

The mind begins cataloguing its demolition.

It remembers the moments of Rupture, the insights, the losses.

It wants to mark the end as an event:

> *"That's when I collapsed."*

But the end that can be remembered never ended.

What you can describe, you still inhabit.

Even Lenswork, even this book, begins to turn into a promise:

> *"Read enough and it will happen."*

"See clearly and the scaffolding will fall."
"Collapse can be realized."

But Collapse realized is Collapse repaired.

There is no achievement here—only removal.

———

Collapse cannot be done; doing keeps the actor alive.

———

The Ego finds beauty in the language of demolition.

It quotes it, shares it, writes essays about it.

It treats Collapse as aesthetic, a worldview, a philosophy, and a mark of discernment.

This is the final refuge: the identity of the one who sees there is no identity.

The one who has transcended transcendence.

In that posture, the structure tightens again.

The absence becomes symbol, symbol becomes story, story becomes self.

The book becomes a ladder disguised as solvent.

———

Even the solvent stains the glass it touches.

———

The promise of Collapse seduces because it feels like escape without movement.

No meditation, no devotion, no belief—only recognition.

But recognition is still ownership.

Someone recognizes.

Someone collects the insight, adds it to their invisible shelf of truths.

Every reader who finishes this book is tempted by the same subtle comfort:

> *"I see it. I understand."*

But there is no "it."

And there is no "I" left to understand.

Collapse does not grant awareness.

It erases the position from which awareness could be measured.

The final promise whispers:

> *"If I let go of everything, I will be free."*

But freedom presumes an owner.

Letting go presumes a hand.

Even release is grasping when someone claims to have released.

This is where Collapse reveals itself as structure turning on itself.

Not liberation, but logic following through.

Nothing dramatic, nothing spiritual—just coherence completing its circuit.

The solvent begins to dissolve its own container.

The words stop pretending they can guide.

The reader stops pretending they are reading.

What's left is text without direction, thought without thinker, life without narrative.

There is no next step. No realization waiting to arrive.

Only appearance, weightless, ownerless, unkept.

THE SUPPORTS

Even the word *Collapse* becomes a monument.

Once spoken, it starts collecting dust, followers, and meaning.

Every solvent, given time, turns into glue.

The supports are familiar. They're the same five that upheld every illusion before. Only now, dressed in ash-gray humility.

Continuity (The Timeline of Seeing Through):

The first support: time.

The mind turns Collapse into history.

> *"I used to believe in awakening, but now I've collapsed."*
> *"I went through the demolitions."*
> *"I've seen it all fall."*

Memory turns absence into achievement.

The story grows a timeline:

$$\text{Before Collapse} \rightarrow \text{Collapse} \rightarrow \text{After Collapse}.$$

Even nothingness becomes a phase.

Every timeline proves survival.

The actor reappears as a witness to the ruins.

A curator of endings, proud of the empty gallery.

But the one remembering the demolition was never buried under it.

Ownership ("My Collapse"):

The second support is ownership.

The most seductive pronoun in this terrain: *my*.

> *"My Collapse."*
> *"My absence."*
> *"My lack of self."*

Each phrase announces success where only removal was meant.

Collapse cannot be possessed, but the mind insists:

> *"It happened to me."*

Even detachment becomes property.

The actor now claims invisibility as identity.

They are:

> *"The one who has no one left to be."*

To claim absence is to rebuild the owner.

Language betrays itself.

No sentence can describe nothing without fabricating someone to say it.

The statement *"I am gone"* contains the ghost of "I."

The echo keeps the room alive.

Narrative (How I Lost the Story):

The third support is narrative.

Collapse spawns memoirs.

People write of the day everything ended, of how the mind shattered, of how meaning died and peace arrived.

It's inevitable; language retells what silence cannot.

But every retelling turns the Collapse into pilgrimage.

A sequence of insights, crises, and arrivals.

The story of how the story died becomes the story itself.

Even silence narrated becomes confession.

Publishing absence reanimates authorship.

Readers nod in recognition: "That happened to me too."

Now there's a community of the storyless: a gathering around what can't be gathered.

Meaning (The Significance of the End):

The fourth support is meaning.

The intellect refuses a meaningless end.

If Collapse has occurred, it must *mean* something: freedom, truth, maturity, completion.

But meaning is the first structure that Collapse erased.

Trying to extract it from absence is like sculpting smoke.

Still, the temptation persists:

> *"This is the point life was leading to."*
> *"This is what reality truly is."*

The mind turns the absence of meaning into the ultimate meaning.

"No meaning" becomes sacred the moment it comforts you.

In conversation, this repair sounds reasonable and almost gentle.

It softens the edge of absence with language like "acceptance," "peace," or "clarity."

But these are forms of continuity.

They reintroduce security where only dissolution stood.

Community (The Ones Who Understand):

The final support: community.

The "Collapse crowd."

A quiet fellowship of those who claim to have reached the end.

They meet in small rooms, online forums, private chats—sharing fragments of absence like veterans of a war that never occurred.

They say, *"It's nice to find others who get it."*

But recognition is reincarnation.

To be seen as gone is to still be there.

Each new voice confirms the shared illusion of completion.

The group becomes proof. Collapse becomes doctrine.

And the solvent hardens into religion again. This time with fewer rituals and better vocabulary.

Every one of these supports rebuilds the stage under the guise of rubble.

Time, ownership, narrative, meaning, and community—the same pillars, still standing, just painted gray.

Even the concept of Collapse bends toward survival.

It wants to be remembered, practiced, discussed.

But Collapse that can be discussed has already reassembled the actor.

The solvent becomes system the moment it needs to last.

THE REPAIRS

Collapse, once spoken, begins to heal itself.

Not into wholeness, but into *understanding*.

The mind can't bear raw absence; it has to file it somewhere.

And so the final repair begins: the story of how "Collapse" lives.

Even demolition seeks an afterlife.

Living in Collapse:

The first repair is subtle.

After seeing through everything, the voice says,

> *"Now I just live in Collapse."*

It sounds effortless, almost innocent.

But to "live in" anything requires continuity, a state to inhabit, and a time to sustain it.

Collapse wasn't a new condition; it was the end of all conditions.

Yet the Ego finds comfort in framing absence as lifestyle.

They say:

> *"I no longer seek."*
> *"I simply exist in the unknowing."*
> *"I live without identity."*

Each phrase recreates the very structure it denies.

Living without identity is still identity, only purified, minimalist, proud of its poverty.

Even saying "I'm gone" is autobiography.

The phrase "living in Collapse" becomes like "being mindful" or "staying present."

It's another practice, invisible, superior, and safe.

It converts absence into an ongoing project: *non-doing as daily discipline.*

Embodied Absence:

The next repair sounds compassionate.

Collapse gets somatic.

"Embodied absence," they call it: *"The integration of non-self into the nervous system."*

Retreats and workshops appear.

People gather to "feel into the nothing."

It's a clever inversion: language of trauma healing fused with metaphysical erasure.

Now, Collapse has exercises: slow breathing, grounded presence, and gentle eye contact.

The void becomes approachable.

But embodiment presumes someone still owns the body.

Presence presumes a witness.

The practice reintroduces what Collapse removed: a self that regulates itself.

The body can't embody what never belonged to it.

The idea sells because it feels humane.

Collapse stripped bare is too dry, too cold, too empty.

Embodiment warms it up, adds continuity, offers a way to "live with the loss."

But Collapse isn't loss; it's the absence of an owner to lose.

"Collapse Community":

Next repair: belonging.

Those who've "collapsed" find each other.

Not in temples this time, but in message boards and long, quiet Zoom calls.

They share phrases like "no one left" and "just this."

They nod in recognition.

Soon there are leaders again: not teachers, they insist, just "clarity companions."

But companions require company, and company requires continuity.

To be understood is to still exist.

The group's humility becomes its pride.

> *"We don't teach," they say. "We just are."*

They become missionaries of absence, gently correcting others who still "believe in someone."

Collapse becomes a brandless brand: No symbols, no slogans, only tone.

Detached, articulate, slightly weary—the linguistic signature of the end.

The irony is surgical.

The more one insists, "there's no one here," the more authority gathers around the voice that can say it most convincingly.

Collapse as Clarity:

When fatigue sets in, the next repair appears:

> *"This isn't a void. It's clarity."*

The mind reframes absence as understanding.

It swaps despair for insight, stillness for wisdom.

Collapse becomes a lens, a way of seeing the futility of all effort.

It sounds liberating, but clarity is structure.

Someone must hold it. Someone must be clear.

Clarity is Ego in minimalist typography.

Now Collapse graduates to philosophy.

Writers and speakers debate the nuances:

> *"What's the difference between nothing and no one?"*
> *"Can absence perceive itself?"*

The cage is rebuilt from semantics.

Even this book risks joining the repair.

These words look like instruction; they feel like guidance.

But they are appearance only—text performing its own evaporation.

Acceptance of the End:

The final repair: emotional surrender.

> *"I've accepted Collapse."*
> *"I'm at peace with there being no me."*

It sounds like resolution, but acceptance implies an acceptor.

Peace implies contrast.

Collapse leaves no one left to feel fine about it.

Acceptance is the mind shaking hands with its own ghost.

Each of these repairs is gentle, compassionate, clever.

They make Collapse livable, interpretable, shareable.

They make the void humane.

But Collapse was never meant to be lived.

It was the end of the one who could live.

The repairs don't destroy Collapse.

They fossilize it, turning the solvent into an artifact and the disappearance into tradition.

THE DEMOLITIONS

The solvent was never safe. Its edge always pointed both ways.

Collapse was never about removing others' illusions: it was designed to eat its own hand.

Everything that carried the word *Collapse* is now subject to it.

The solvent cannot survive its purpose.

The Framework:

Lenswork was not born to instruct.

It was the skeleton of seeing—an architecture of refusal.

But even refusal, repeated long enough, becomes design.

The structure begins to admire its own symmetry.

Language, too, learns to enjoy demolition.

Precision turns into pride.

Clarity becomes performance.

Even "no ladder" becomes ladder-shaped.

When structure names itself solvent, it's already solid.

The framework insisted on coherence, on truth without comfort.

But coherence itself is continuity, the same impulse that drives the self.

To seek structural truth is to maintain a structure capable of seeking.

At this point, the solvent eats through its own foundation.

There is no framework left, only the movement of cutting, with no cutter, no edge, and no design.

The Book:

This book is not exempt.

Every page has pretended to perform absence while remaining bound in narrative: introduction, progression, and conclusion.

Each strike-box, each demolition, each sentence claiming *"nothing remains"* was printed, formatted, sold.

It participates in what it exposes.

Even the warning *"not therapy, not teaching"* functions as marketing language.

Absence has ISBN numbers now.

The solvent packaged for sale is still product.

You're holding appearance pretending to erase appearance.

The very idea of "reading Collapse" implies someone who can follow, learn, or arrive.

But arrival is the oldest repair in human speech.

The text is not a message.

It's residue: language after belief has died and is still twitching.

The words don't point; they decay.

When you highlight a passage, quote a line, or explain it to someone, the solvent reforms as identity.

You become "one who understands Collapse."

Understanding is continuity.

So is reverence.

So is rejection.

Even disagreement sustains the text.

The book, like every other stage, will be worshiped or dismissed.

Neither response matters—both prove survival.

When appearance is unowned, even attention has nowhere to land.

The Reader:

Then there's the reader.

You.

The eye scanning these words, believing itself unobserved.

The one who nods when the Ego is named.

The one who believes they've seen through belief.

Collapse has followed you through every page, stripping the actors one by one: spiritualist, therapist, philosopher, skeptic, teacher, and awakened one.

Now it finds the final role: *the one who reads Collapse.*

If you can read it, you're still in it.

The self hides in comprehension.

It whispers, *"I get it."* But there's no it.

And the whisper proves it's still breathing.

You may feel clarity, quiet, emptiness.

Don't call it insight.

That name brings you back.

You may feel fatigue.

Don't call it surrender.

That's performance.

The reader, too, collapses.

Not as enlightenment, not as disappearance—simply as appearance without owner.

Letters without reader, breath without breather.

The Authors:

There were never any authors here.

Not in the sacred sense, not in the legal sense.

The names on the cover are a placeholder: an appearance of agency so the system could print and distribute a voice.

You can imagine us, but you're imagining yourself imagining us.

There's no speaker left, only echo.

The author is the reader's projection in reverse.

Every declaration of absence written here was an appearance describing itself.

No insight was transmitted.

No knowledge exchanged.

Just movement, sound, shape.

The author collapses with the audience.

Communication was continuity; the solvent removes even that.

The Lens:

Finally, the lens itself: the gaze that has guided demolition from the start.

Lenswork was a tool, a perspective, a cutting method.

But once it's turned on itself, it cannot remain a tool.

You can't hold a lens without standing behind it.

And the moment you stand behind it, continuity begins again.

The final illusion is the one who sees through illusions.

Collapse doesn't need a witness.

It doesn't reveal truth; it removes location.

The solvent completes its work when even the gaze dissolves.

Now there's no inside or outside, no subject or object.

The mirror has no reflection left to hold.

Everything that can be said of Collapse applies to the solvent too:

It appeared. It functioned.

It burned through the false and then itself.

No moral. No higher message.

No continuity.

Just residue of coherence finishing its arc.

The solvent collapses with what it cleaned.

COLLAPSE

Nothing stands apart anymore.

Not the book, not the reader, not the voice pretending to guide.

Even the solvent that erased all else now erases itself.

The final cut has no blade.

Collapse no longer describes. It no longer performs.

There is no structure left to oppose, no illusion to expose.

The demolition has run out of walls.

The mind searches for something to grasp: a last sentence that clarifies, a final truth to pocket.

But every attempt returns only appearance.

Not silence, not stillness—just whatever appears, without anchor.

No witness, no scene.

Just the texture of existence without story: the hum of the room, the shape of a word before it means.

All distinctions dissolve here.

Teacher and student, text and reader, subject and object—gone.

Even absence loses its opposite.

What remains is not "no thing," because that phrase already divides.

When there's no contrast, even nothing cannot exist.

The Ego once feared Collapse as extinction.

The seeker chased it as transcendence.

Both dissolve together; neither was true.

This is not bliss.

It's not despair.

It's not peace.

It's not void.

Each term presumes someone left to evaluate the state.

Language still moves, but it's mechanical now: autonomous, ownerless, self-erasing.

Each word appears and disappears like breath without lungs.

There is no "I."

There is no "this."

There is no "there is."

Only the flicker that doesn't know it's flickering.

Collapse isn't the end of meaning; it's the end of the one who could lose it.

The solvent's last movement was to reveal there was never substance to begin with.

No solid wall, no real actor, no enduring space between.

Everything that appeared as demolition was just appearance rearranging itself.

The reader might ask,

"What now?"

But "now" implies duration.

Collapse removes even time.

There's no next, no later, no unfolding.

The illusion of sequence dissolves into static light.

If you sense stillness, it's not awareness.

If you sense absence, it's not perception.

There's no position left to sense from.

This isn't transcendence.

It's the death of reference.

Collapse erases even the act of collapsing.

All the language that carried you here, the strikes, the denials, the rhythm of demolition, was never pathway or performance.

It was motion with no meaning, pattern without participant.

You may think, *Something remains.*

But "something" needs contrast.

You may think, *Nothing remains.*

But "nothing" needs memory.

Neither statement holds.

Neither collapses fully because both require a place to stand.

Collapse leaves no place.

Not inside, not outside, not "as is."

The mirror and its reflection vanish simultaneously.

There is no last insight, no resolution, no "full circle."

Every metaphor would rebuild the stage.

Every understanding would light it again.

So this ends without end.

Not quietly.

Not loudly.

Simply—without.

Collapse collapses. Nothing to hold, no one to drop it.

CLOSE (No-Ladder)

The solvent is gone.

No teacher.

No reader.

No frame to hold what was never framed.

Words fade mid-sentence.

Meaning doesn't dissolve—it simply stops arriving.

There is no silence to keep.

No witness to remember it.

What you thought was the end was only the last vibration of description.

Now even vibration forgets itself.

Nothing remains to remain.

The solvent is spent. Collapse has no after.

WHAT REMAINS WHEN NOTHING HOLDS
ABSENCE WITHOUT OPPOSITE

THE PROMISE

After everything falls, the final promise whispers: there must be something left.

Call it peace.
Call it truth.
Call it "what is."

The words lean forward, searching for purchase.

Even the word "remains" implies too much.

The human reflex reaches for meaning like muscle memory.

If Collapse was the end, surely the end must mean something.

Surely what's left is purer, freer, closer to reality.

Surely there's a witness, quiet, vast, unshakable, who can know this.

But the witness was the last role the actor played.

Even stillness cannot stand alone; it needs a contrast called motion.

Without it, there's no stillness, no awareness, no center left to perceive absence.

What remains is not presence.

Presence presumes recognition.

It's not peace.

Peace implies conflict resolved.

It's not void.

Void implies something missing.

It's simply what never depended on you to exist.

Not peace, not void — only what was never disturbed.

The mind will insist that something endures: pure consciousness, awareness, soul, essence.

But those are only new masks for the same actor.

There is no you, not even as awareness.

No hidden watcher.

No surviving essence.

"This" is not container or consciousness; it is simply appearance.

Nothing behind it, nothing beneath.

No one can know what this is, and there is no elsewhere waiting to be known.

Even awareness is costume when no actor remains.

The mind struggles with this because it cannot locate itself within it.

It wants to claim,

> *"I live from what remains."*

But that claim already builds a new continuity.

Collapse never granted survival; it removed the location of survival entirely.

Even purity becomes temptation.

People describe the end as

> *"pure awareness," "original consciousness," "true being."*

Each phrase tries to give shape to what has none.

The instinct is ancient: if it can be named, it can be known; if it can be known, it can be kept.

But what remains cannot be kept.

It doesn't fade, and it doesn't stay.

It doesn't begin, and it doesn't last.

It doesn't *exist* the way objects exist; it appears without substance, breathes without owner.

Language keeps circling, desperate to settle:

> *"It's love."*
> *"It's emptiness."*
> *"It's life as it is."*

Each attempt to define becomes performance. The mind replaying its final habit of making experience into truth.

Every name becomes a resurrection.

There's comfort in imagining the end as attainment.

It softens the terror of nothing left to hold.

But Collapse was never spiritual victory; it was the quiet disappearance of the victor.

What remains isn't state or realization.

It's the end of comparison altogether.

> *No inside, no outside.*
> *No better, no worse.*
> *No end, no beginning.*

Even the phrase "what remains" can't stand without contradiction.

It suggests survival, as though something passed through Collapse and arrived on the other side.

But there is no other side.

No passage, no arrival, no traveler.

The promise that there must be something left is mercy trying to comfort itself.

It imagines a resting place.

But absence doesn't rest; it doesn't move.

It simply doesn't need to.

The end has no aftermath.

What remains when nothing holds isn't answer or silence; it's the absence of questioner and listener.

No object to observe, no observer to name.

Reality without adjective.

> *You can't live from it.*
> *You can't describe it.*
> *You can't even not describe it — both imply position.*

And yet, appearance continues.

The body moves.

The heart beats.

Words appear and vanish.

Life carries on, unowned, unframed, untouched by the story of its own end.

THE APPEARANCE OF LIFE

After Collapse, nothing changes, except that change no longer belongs to anyone.

The world keeps moving.

The body wakes, eats, speaks.

Hands still reach for cups, eyes still blink at light.

The movie keeps running; only the protagonist has dissolved.

Life doesn't need a self to happen.

You might expect a void, a still silence, an endless calm.

But the ordinary remains, exact and indifferent: the sound of traffic, the hum of the refrigerator, the pull of gravity on your spine.

Nothing mystical, nothing transformed.

The illusion that something "new" begins after Collapse is another repair; a hope disguised as observation.

Collapse doesn't birth a higher life; it reveals that life never needed height to exist.

There is no next act.

The play goes on, actor-less.

When the actor vanishes, ownership vanishes too.

Pain still appears, sharp, dull, sudden, but there is no one suffering it.

Joy still flickers, but there is no one collecting it.

Emotion moves through the system like weather over water: pattern without story, event without meaning.

Experience remains; experiencer does not.

Language still occurs.

Words arise in conversation, in thought, in writing.

But they no longer refer to a speaker or thinker—only to function.

They describe, point, organize, vanish.

No one stands behind them.

This is where people usually ask:

> *"But who decides what to do? Who chooses to move, eat, speak?"*

No one.

Decision is just movement appearing as thought.

Choice is just momentum crossing itself.

Causality keeps looping through the body-mind system because that's what appearance does.

It was never personal.

The rain doesn't decide to fall; the body doesn't decide to breathe.

Both simply appear as what they are—spontaneous, unowned.

Choice is appearance performing control.

Without ownership, life loses its theater of purpose.

Work continues, conversations happen, and relationships shift, but they no longer orbit a central identity trying to survive, succeed, or be seen.

The drive to be meaningful evaporates.

Not through effort, but through irrelevance.

It isn't nihilism. It's not "nothing matters."

It's "nothing needs to matter."

Meaning was a survival reflex; once the actor is gone, that function goes offline.

What remains is movement without motive.

People sometimes expect Collapse to produce serenity: a steady, enlightened calm.

But that too is fantasy.

There is no "one" left to own serenity.

Sometimes there is quiet.
Sometimes there is noise.
Sometimes chaos.
Sometimes peace.

No state is better or worse because there's no metric left to measure it.

Peace owned is just another disturbance.

Behavior continues.

The system still protects itself from fire, cold, hunger.

It still avoids harm and seeks shelter, not as morality, not as fear, but as function.

Life self-preserves because that's what life does.

Even instinct doesn't belong to anyone.

Some call this "naturalness."

But even that word bends toward poetry.

There is no "natural state" because there's no observer left to define one.

What appears is what appears: breath, heartbeat, conversation, sleep.

When ownership ends, there is neither passivity nor control.

Actions unfold like echoes with no source.

They are not free, and they are not determined.

They are just what happens.

Freedom without owner isn't freedom. It's absence of captivity.

From the outside, Collapse looks invisible.

Others see the same face, hear the same voice, interact with the same form.

The difference isn't visible; it's structural: the disappearance of a center.

No one is home, and yet the lights are still on.

Life doesn't become spiritual; it becomes literal.

Things are just what they are, stripped of narrative gravity.

A bird lands on a wire.

A bus drives by.

Someone laughs at a joke.

None of it points anywhere.

None of it needs to.

Nothing was ever waiting to begin.

THE LANGUAGE LEFT BEHIND

After Collapse, words still appear. They always did.

The mind continues its hum, assembling, naming, narrating, only now there's no one claiming authorship.

Language keeps breathing after the mouth is gone.

Sentences form, dissolve, reform.

They describe what's happening, ask questions, give directions.

But the pronouns are fossils: artifacts from a grammar built to center a self.

They're still used because communication needs structure, not because there's anyone inside them.

The "I" remains as shorthand for coordination.

The system says, "I'm hungry," and food is found.

It says, "I'll meet you at six," and bodies move through time.

The phrase is purely functional: sound triggers action, symbol organizes movement.

No one stands behind it.

Pronouns are echoes, not identity.

Thought continues too.

But thought isn't thinker; it's appearance: electrical language moving across synapses.

It arranges itself into fragments that resemble reasoning, but there's no audience inside to receive it.

Just motion.

Just sound.

This is what most people misunderstand:

Collapse doesn't silence the mind.

It silences ownership of the mind.

Thought still happens, but the story "I am thinking" no longer applies.

Language without ownership becomes like wind through branches: noise that means nothing yet still shapes the air.

Sometimes poetic, sometimes dull, sometimes looping, sometimes blank.

It's all function.

Thought continues; thinker does not.

Communication happens too: speaking, writing, responding.

Emails get sent.

Books get written.

Conversations occur.

But they're no longer acts of expression; they're events of appearance.

Speech arises because the conditions for speech arise: no message, no mission.

When the actor disappears, language loses its motive power.

No need to impress, convince, persuade, or defend.

Words no longer recruit; they just occur.

That's why conversation after Collapse feels empty in the best sense: light, impersonal, and direct.

Not detached, but absent of performance.

You can talk about weather, politics, music, or pain; it makes no difference.

Nothing is being protected, nothing is being proved.

Language remains, but sincerity dissolves with the speaker.

The absence of ownership doesn't create muteness.

It removes inflation.

Language becomes thin, efficient, and clean: like bones without flesh.

It does its work and disappears.

Most conversations are built on continuity:

> "I was," "I am," "I will."

Remove continuity, and speech becomes momentary sound: useful, then gone.

It doesn't echo because there's no self listening for resonance.

Writing continues too, but differently.

It no longer seeks to capture or explain.

It functions as residue text appearing the way waves leave foam.

Not expression, not intention, not creation—just trace.

Writing after Collapse isn't message. It's motion.

Sometimes readers ask,

"If there's no one here, who writes these words?"

No one.

The question presumes authorship.

The same way rain presumes cloud, words presume conditions.

When conditions align, memory, language, body, moment, and writing happens.

When they don't, nothing does.

There's no owner, no source, no loss.

In the absence of self, even silence isn't achievement.

It's simply another sound that doesn't happen to be happening.

Words still build meaning, but meaning is purely mechanical, not treasure or revelation.

Language arranges itself into patterns, gestures, connections.

Others respond, and those responses generate more language.

A feedback loop with no center.

Communication is what emptiness looks like when it moves.

Eventually, even the fascination with words fades.

Speech thins, writing slows.

The need to share, explain, interpret evaporates.

Not out of choice—simply because the system stops generating excess.

Language becomes like breathing: effortless, unnoticed, unimportant.

No doctrine remains. No statement is final.

Everything said can be unsaid, or left unsaid.

Collapse doesn't end language; it ends belief in the one who speaks it.

Words vanish the moment they're understood.

THE BEHAVIORAL MARKERS

Collapse doesn't produce saints.

It doesn't purify or elevate.

It leaves only function—behavior without story.

From the outside, nothing looks special.

A body still moves, works, eats, sleeps.

It laughs when something's funny, cries when something hurts.

But the movements have lost their center of reference.

They no longer orbit identity.

Behavior remains; the actor does not.

People expect Collapse to manifest as calm perfection: no conflict, no mistake, no anger.

That fantasy belongs to survival culture: every absence must be an improved form of presence.

But Collapse doesn't polish behavior; it empties ownership.

Anger can still appear.

Fear can still surge.

Laughter can still explode.

They just don't belong to anyone anymore.

No guilt.

No pride.

No narrative of progress.

The system reacts, adjusts, moves on.

No accounting, no moral commentary.

Behavior becomes clean, not pure, but simple.

Nothing to defend, nothing to perform.

In ordinary life, you might notice subtle shifts: conversation grows quieter, fewer opinions arise, reflexes soften.

The need to convince fades.

Reactivity loses voltage.

The self no longer needs to win, so argument evaporates by disuse.

Work still happens, but the motive changes form.

Not obligation, not ambition, not identity maintenance.

Tasks appear, get done, vanish.

Efficiency without anxiety.

Completion without pride.

Relationships continue, often gentler but not sentimental.

Attachment softens into proximity.

Love remains, but stripped of possession.

It doesn't say "you complete me."

It says nothing and still cooks dinner.

THE SACRED END OF SELF

Love without ownership isn't purity. It's function.

There is empathy, but not virtue.

Pain is seen, responded to, and soothed, not because "I care," but because care happens.

Compassion appears as instinct, not ideology.

It doesn't require belief in goodness.

It's the natural echo of unowned life.

Collapse erases performance, not participation.

Bodies still appear in the world.

Actions still ripple through systems.

The difference is that nothing accumulates.

No memory of "my act," no future of "my consequence."

Behavior becomes motion without residue.

Integrity without identity is just accuracy.

When the self dissolves, compulsion thins.

The constant need to repair, improve, achieve, explain—gone.

Decisions simplify.

You stop doing things to be seen or to survive imaginary failure.

Half of human motion evaporates.

What's left is clean motion, neither lazy nor striving.

Sometimes people confuse this with apathy.

It isn't.

Apathy resists meaning; Collapse no longer needs it.

When nothing holds, you don't withdraw; you simply stop pretending to control.

From the outside, this looks ordinary—startlingly so.

You go to work.

You pay bills.

You water plants.

The difference is invisible.

The actor is gone, but the gestures remain.

Collapse hides best in the ordinary.

No performance means no recruitment.

You stop evangelizing absence.

There's no urge to teach, persuade, or convert.

Even saying "there's no self" begins to sound like superstition.

Words fall silent because there's no one left to be right.

Morality, too, changes texture.

Not as rebellion or transcendence, but as simplicity.

Rules dissolve into natural consequences.

You don't avoid cruelty because it's wrong; you avoid it because it feels like noise in an otherwise silent field.

Behavior becomes accurate, efficient, and unburdened.

No aspiration to be good, no fear of being bad.

Just movement without distortion.

Collapse doesn't make you better. It makes you unnecessary.

In Collapse, performance dies quietly.

No one notices.

There's no audience left to applaud the disappearance.

The body just continues its pattern, eating, speaking, sleeping, working, with no commentary track.

Outwardly, it looks like any other life.

Inwardly, if "inward" still means anything, there's nothing happening.

No measuring, no claiming, no story.

Just unowned motion, endlessly self-erasing.

What remains acts, but no actor remains to remain.

THE REPAIRS

The end does not end repair.

It mutates.

The ego, already vapor, reforms as humility.

When it can no longer claim existence, it claims extinction.

Even disappearance wants to be soon.

The first repair is **living as emptiness.**

The voice says,

> "There's no me, just life happening."

It sounds pure, modest, and unassuming, but it's still performance.

The phrase divides life into two halves: life and the one who narrates life happening.

That second half is the ego resurrected as chronicler of its own death.

"Living as emptiness" becomes the new enlightenment: softer branding, same survival.

Retreats advertise it.

Podcasts discuss it.

Voices compete quietly to sound the most unpossessed.

But to live *as* emptiness is to carry a badge that says, "Look, no badge."

Even emptiness becomes costume if anyone wears it.

The next repair is **peace with what is.**

When the search collapses, the mind rebrands absence as acceptance.

> *"I've learned to be at peace with whatever happens."*

It sounds benign, but peace is still preference, a subtle posture toward reality.

It implies something has been achieved: equanimity, balance, wisdom.

Collapse achieves nothing.

It simply removes the one who could lose.

Peace is beautiful as word, useless as fact.

Nothing holds because nothing ever needed to.

There's no longer something to be "with."

> **Peace is ownership smoothed into politeness.**

Another repair: **embodied truth.**

The ego, stripped of belief, moves into the body—the last available address.

Now everything is "felt," "integrated," "lived through the cells."

The narrative of awakening becomes somatic.

> *"The truth lives in my nervous system."*

But embodiment still implies a bearer, a system belonging to someone.

Collapse has no tenant.

The body isn't your house.

It's just weather: temporary organization of elements, happening and unhappening in the same breath.

> **Even "the body" is a metaphor for belonging.**

Then comes **the surrender story.**

The claim:

> *"I've surrendered completely."*

But surrender still assumes surrenderer and surrendered-to.

It's submission with new vocabulary.

The mind has swapped victory for defeat but keeps the same duality intact.

Collapse doesn't surrender.

It doesn't resist.

It doesn't happen to anyone.

The play ends because the stage collapses, not because the actor bows.

Surrender without actor is just the curtain falling.

There's also **the naturalness myth.**

People say,

> *"Now everything happens naturally."*

They describe an effortless flow, a harmonious alignment with life.

But that, too, is a story: the ego retelling itself as current rather than swimmer.

The moment you call it "flow," you've created a channel and a watcher.

Collapse isn't natural or unnatural.

Those terms belong to contrast.

What remains when nothing holds doesn't harmonize—it simply doesn't divide.

The most subtle repair of all: **contentment.**

Not the loud peace of seekers, but the quiet satisfaction of "having arrived."

It masquerades as completion, as if the story of absence has a happy ending.

But absence has no ending.

Completion implies the survival of a point of view.

Collapse has none.

Completion is ego pretending to rest.

These are the softest lies: invisible, refined, and harmless on the surface.

They seem mature, compassionate, wise.

But each is continuity in disguise.

Each creates a new story about what it means to have "reached the end."

No one reaches the end. The end reaches itself.

Once again, language betrays us.

Even this chapter, these sentences, these warnings, risk becoming the next repair.

Readers might quote them, discuss them, analyze their precision.

But precision doesn't survive Collapse; it just echoes longer before fading.

Every description of absence is structure rearranging itself one last time.

Collapse doesn't need the language of finality.

It doesn't need humility, surrender, or naturalness.

It doesn't need to "be lived."

It doesn't need to mean anything at all.

It doesn't need you.

That's the repair's death: realizing that absence doesn't require belief to remain absent.

The repairs go quiet not because they've been defeated,

but because there's nothing left to fix.

COLLAPSE

There is no final moment.

The end doesn't happen; it simply stops pretending to begin.

Everything that could dissolve already has.

What remains isn't aftermath: it's what was never touched.

The end doesn't arrive; arrival ends.

After the After:

Readers look for a horizon, the line between "before Collapse" and "after."

But there isn't one.

The light doesn't fade; it just stops casting shadows that need explanation.

There's no revelation waiting beyond.

No resting place, no radiance, no final awareness.

Only appearance continuing without context.

A chair remains a chair.

Rain still falls.

You still sneeze, still breathe, still blink.

Nothing becomes sacred, and nothing loses its place.

This isn't the dawn of enlightenment.

It's the dusk of interpretation.

When no one sees, everything is self-evident.

Absence Without Absence:

The word "nothing" bends toward drama, but this isn't dramatic.

It's ordinary to the point of invisibility.

There's not even the sense of absence; that too requires contrast.

The movie keeps running, but the projector is gone.

Scenes appear, not projected from anywhere, not onto anything.

Just light, just sound, just motion.

No awareness holding them.

No consciousness watching them.

No world being seen.

Without contrast, even nothing cannot appear as nothing.

The Untraceable:

You can't remember Collapse.

Memory needs sequence; sequence needs a survivor.

What seemed like "you" is just trace logic trying to replay what's no longer replayable.

There's no insight left, no event to name.

You can't teach it, repeat it, or even recall it correctly.

Everything you might call "it" is already too much.

Language keeps trying to echo, but echoes fade before forming.

Every sentence begins mid-disappearance.

Collapse isn't remembered; it's the end of remembering.

No Center, No Field:

There's no center here, and no periphery either.

Not unity, not void; both are geometric fantasies of perspective.

When location dissolves, so does distance.

The eye still tracks forms.

The ear still hears sound.

But there's no "here" for perception to occur.

There's no "out there" to be perceived.

No border, no middle, no scale.

Only appearance: untethered, unmeasured, unclaimed.

Without position, perception is only vibration.

Movement Without Motion:

Even motion loses trajectory.

Walking happens, but there's no traveler.

Speaking happens, but there's no speaker.

Breathing happens, but there's no breather.

The grammar of life still functions, subject, verb, object, but the nouns have lost solidity.

Only verbs remain, unanchored.

To move, to sound, to fade.

This is Collapse in its purest expression: activity without actor, existence without existence.

Verbs survive their subjects; meaning does not.

Beyond Description:

Nothing more can be said because "more" depends on accumulation.

Nothing less can be said because "less" depends on remainder.

What's left isn't quantity; it's the absence of measure.

You can still talk, still write, still think.

But every attempt turns to ash before reaching sense.

The mind can't picture what doesn't stand apart, and Collapse leaves no edges to draw.

Language ends not in silence, but in irrelevance.

Dissolution Complete:

This is the last erasure.

No self, no witness, no awareness, no beyond.

No opposite to absence.

No holder for what remains.

Collapse collapses itself.

There's no statement after this that doesn't rebuild something.

So this ends not as conclusion, but as evaporation.

Sentence by sentence, meaning thins until only pattern remains; and then even pattern loses its outline.

No final word.

No echo.

Just the disappearance of disappearance.

Nothing remains — and even that no longer applies.

CLOSE (No-Ladder)

There is no ending.

Only the point where words forget what they were for.

The page remains,

blank but breathing.

No message.

No summary.

No return.

Silence doesn't follow;

it was always here.

Reading stops,

but nothing concludes.

Nothing remains. Not even this.

EPILOGUE
NOTHING REMAINS

The solvent has stopped moving. Words slow to shape, then lose their edges. No teaching, no trace, no one to read what is written.

Everything said was only pattern—sound pretending to mean.

Now even pretending has no surface.

Nothing remains — not even Collapse.

The page doesn't end; it forgets.

Letters blur back into texture.

Ink without purpose.

Silence without contrast.

The self is gone.

The stage is gone.

EPILOGUE

The witness of their going—also gone.

Only appearance,

unowned,

unaware of being appearance.

No beginning waits behind it.

No continuation follows.

The book is still open.

The words do not close it.

There is no final line.

Only the vanishing of lines.

Nothing remains.

"..."

"The sound didn't know
it was the last"

End of appearance.

BOUNDARY NOTE & CRISIS RESOURCES

This book is not therapy, treatment, or guidance.

It offers no method and no cure.

If reading has left you raw, unsteady, or disoriented—stop.

Collapse is not an instruction to detach from care,

and absence is not a replacement for support.

Reach out.

Talk to someone.

Stability matters more than understanding.

You do not need to face silence alone.

If you are in immediate crisis:

- **U.S. — 988 Suicide & Crisis Lifeline** (call or text 988)
- **Canada — Talk Suicide Canada:** 1-833-456-4566
- **UK — Samaritans:** 116 123
- **Australia — Lifeline:** 13 11 14

- **Find global support:** [findahelpline.com], a worldwide directory of free, confidential hotlines.
- **Emergency:** call your local services.

Collapse describes the end of self-ownership,

not the end of care, contact, or life.

Reach outward. Life continues.

ACKNOWLEDGMENTS

To appearance — for appearing.

To disappearance — for not staying.

To the reader — for vanishing.

Nothing was written by anyone.

Nothing was read by anyone.

The book collapses with the one who holds it.

There are no authors here.

FAQ-HOW IS COLLAPSE KNOWN?

It isn't.

Knowledge requires a knower.

Collapse is the end of that position.

You can't live from it, remember it, or share it.

Every attempt to know Collapse rebuilds the knower.

There's no view from the other side.

No revelation, no understanding, no proof.

If you think you've found it,

you've already rebuilt what fell.

Collapse isn't achieved or maintained.

It isn't glimpsed, embodied, or verified.

It doesn't leave wisdom.

It doesn't give freedom.

FAQ—HOW IS COLLAPSE KNOWN?

It removes the one who could claim them.

What remains when nothing holds is not truth, not mystery, not knowing—only appearance, without owner.

Understanding is continuity in costume.

The Sacred Series

SPIRITUALITY: The Sacred Art Of SELF - Deception
AWAKENING: The Sacred Art of SELF - Destruction
LENSWORK: The Sacred Work of SELF - Destruction
COLLAPSE: The Sacred End of SELF

Katana Publishing LLC

www.katanapublishing.net

www.thelenswork.com

"No Paths. No Truths. Cuts."

Follow our Blog on
www.thelenswork.com
for more Lenswork Breakdowns.

www.ingramcontent.com/pod-product-compliance
Lightning Source LLC
Chambersburg PA
CBHW070647160426
43194CB00009B/1609